Starting Your Own

SHOP

All you need to know to open a successful shop

MATT THOMAS

crimson

This edition first published in Great Britain 2008 by
Crimson Publishing, a division of Crimson Business Ltd
Westminster House
Kew Road
Richmond
Surrey
TW9 2ND

A catalogue record for this book is available from the British Library.

ISBN 978 1 85458 435 9

Printed and bound by Mega Print, Istanbul

Contents

Introduction

➡ SO YOU WANT TO OPEN A SHOP. . .

And it's easy to see why! Running your own shop can be one of the most rewarding and sociable ways to live your working life and potentially make your fortune in the process. It holds equal appeal to the fiercest of empire-building entrepreneurs as it does families, couples and ambition-shy one man bands whose chief driver is quality of life.

Napoleon's disparaging dismissal of Britain as a 'nation of shopkeepers' is no more a smear than an observation that shops are a strictly British passion, but what is clear is that despite an increasingly difficult economic climate and the growing dominance of all-encompassing supermarket chains our passion for independent shops has far from abated.

Indeed, while perhaps not reflected with equal gusto economically, the rise in consumer demand for ethically and locally sourced products has seen a renewed vigour for the independent shop serving its local communities and niche markets.

It's true we many never see a return of the Arkwright general store and proud-aproned shopkeeper to every street corner, but there's a progressive movement of small independent shops finding new ways to compete against the big brands that once threatened their existence.

The new wave of small shops are looking beyond the desperate scramble for best price and focussing on providing value in other forms. Personalised, superior customer service is all too often redundant in faceless homogenous 50 check-out stores. Niche offerings providing a wider range of specialised goods, presented by staff who are knowledgeable about the subjects are a real find.

At the other end of the spectrum, globalisation and international trade have opened the door to whole continents of suppliers providing products, services and manufacturing labour at prices that offer the true entrepreneur mouth-watering mark-up opportunities. As wholesalers and importers exploit this by the carton, so the supply chain flows deeper and closer to even the most modest of start-ups.

The web continues to revolutionise retail but multi-channel selling has replaced a one-way flow to online trading, and the value of physical shops has been somewhat resurrected. Yes, shops come with overheads and greater barriers to entry but there's no escaping the fact they remain dear to the UK consumer who likes to buy in person as well as online or by mail order. Touching and feeling products and face-to-face interaction can't be replicated, while shops are extensions of their owners' personalities, offering experiences the web can't.

Starting in a downturn

There's no escaping the economic downturn and now daily declines in trading figures for some of the UK's largest retailers as commentators predict we're spiralling towards recession. Cause to think again about starting-up? If you're asking that question, then possibly so. It's true, starting any business, let alone retail, in the current climate and with banks' cutting back on lending is a real challenge. However, what sets successful business owners aside from those that fail is a determination and flexibility to adapt to the environment around them. What sets aside entrepreneurs is an unerring resilience and belief to make it happen regardless of outside forces.

It's a simple fact that there's never a bad time to start a good business and providing you're realistic about the sales you can reasonably expect and margins you can make, there's no reason why your shop can't succeed. What's more, it can prosper as the economy recovers, which it eventually will.

A downturn can also be used to your advantage. Commercial leases have dropped by around 15% in the last 12 months, cushioning the reduction of lending options with reduced overheads. While it's not pleasant to see, big companies shedding staff has also flooded the recruitment market with previously unaffordable skilled workers that can make a real difference to the success of your business.

This book

Whatever your motivation for opening a shop, be it to simply achieve better work-life balance or the first step towards rivalling Philip Green's grip on the retail hierarchy, we've packed this book with practical hands-on advice for you to not just read, but act on.

The book is structured to take you through the journey of opening a shop from concept to planning, raising finance, finding premises and suppliers, generating interest for your opening to the minute you finally flick the open sign.

But we don't desert you there as almost every other business book and support service does with the promise of a fairytale ending. We've a whole section on what really happens when you start trading: and we deal with the reality. The harsh truth is that the first six months will almost certainly be an emotional rollercoaster containing more lows than highs as you struggle to establish your business and cope with pitfalls of disappointing early sales, resultant negative cashflow and the whole host of unexpected problems that inevitably occur.

How do we know it's the reality? Well because we've asked the people that know far better than we do: real entrepreneurs that have been there and done it and are going through it now. From the a retail veteran who's sat on the boards of three of the UK's top retail brands to a true entrepreneur who started by selling his car and lying to his credit card company but came out on top and is now sitting pretty after selling for in excess of £200m. We're more than aware most of you don't aspire to operate on such a scale though, that's why we've roped in a company that only started trading this year, one that's running a shop and Post Office in a combined space of 400 sq ft and an expanding two store fashion boutique.

We've structured the book so it can be used either as a chronological guide or as a flick-through tool that can be dipped into at any point of the journey with clear, independent advice, top tips and the inside track from our shop owners on what they did in every scenario.

As one of our experts sums up brilliantly, starting a shop is risky, hugely challenging and 'bloody hard work' but packed with all sorts of life-fulfilling rewards. Enjoy it and, you never know, you could end up making for your fortune as well.

Case studies

These experts have been there and done it, and turned their retail businesses into a sensation. Mike Clare began his bed business in 1987, and now has more than 170 stores to his name; John Spooner was crucial in expanding high-street stores Monsoon and Accessorize, until their eventual flotation for £352m. Read about their experiences here, and benefit from their expert advice throughout the book.

These businesses may not be household names, but they are certainly well positioned to give their advice on opening a shop. All have opened in the past four years, and are now well established within their communities. These are shops you should aspire to be like within a year of opening, and they've got some great advice to help you along the way.

FROM THE EXPERTS:
Mike Clare

Experience: Founder of Dreams plc

Mike Clare is executive chairman and founder of Dreams plc, Britain's leading bed specialist. Dreams has grown from Mike's first bed shop based in Uxbridge in 1987 and now boasts more than 170 superstores throughout the UK with a turnover in excess of £200m.

Having expanded the business at a rate of over 30% p.a. for the previous five years and collecting the Ernst & Young's Entrepreneur of the Year Award in 2002, Mike sold his controlling stake in Dreams in March 2008 for a reported £200m.

A celebrated retailer and entrepreneur, Mike is a Liveryman of The Worshipful Company of Furniture Makers, a Freeman of the City of London, President of the Furnishing Trades Benevolent Association, Board Director (Non Exec) of the British Retail Consortium and Trustee of The Buckinghamshire Foundation.

Mike worked his way up through the management ranks of retail furniture companies such as Williams, Hardy's and Perrings and tried his hand with a number of home-based businesses before taking the plunge with Dreams, then The Sofa Bed Centre, in 1986. 'I was always coming up with little business ideas to make money,' says Mike. 'While at college, I used to buy massive boxes of condoms and then sell them to the other students individually for twice the price. I've just always loved the excitement of trading.'

After leaving college at 18 with a business diploma, Mike started working for a furniture retailer in the beds department and gradually clawed his way up to managerial level. 'If I'd landed a job in the carpet department I'd probably be the leading carpet retailer now,' he jokes.

At the age of 30, with a pregnant wife at home, he decided he'd had enough of being an employee. 'I found a small store in Uxbridge that was in a terrible state, but the rent was cheap. I worked out I needed about £25,000 to startup. I had about £1,500 of my own cash, and sold my car to raise some more. I borrowed some on my credit card and told them it was for a kitchen refurbishment.'

He scraped together £10,000 and the bank matched it. 'Once I raised the £20,000 I thought, "well the suppliers will just have to wait a bit for their money". A lot of people don't like the idea of starting a business in debt but sometimes you've just got to take that risk and work hard.'

Within two years of starting The Sofa Bed Centre, Mike had opened a further three stores. But despite having progressed this far he took the decision to expand outside of sofa beds

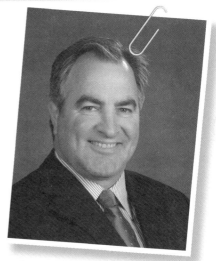

and rebrand. 'We had a choice between selling sofas and selling beds. Beds took up less space so we could stock more. Also people aren't as fussy about the look of a bed. They're easier to sell – so that's what we went with.' He changed the company name to Dreams against the advice of his accountant who warned it didn't say what the company did – 'That's why you're an accountant and I'm an entrepreneur', was Mike's simple answer – and he hasn't looked back since.

He describes the early nineties as Dreams' most difficult time. 'There was a bit of a recession and we did struggle but we got through it.' Developing a successful formula was the key, although Mike admits it wasn't a strategic approach as such. 'I would look for a new store that was to let and negotiate really hard with the landlord. We'd order the stock, have a grand opening, get a cake in the shape of a bed, invite the mayor to the launch, then move on to the next site. It wasn't really a plan, we just did it.'

While Mike didn't plan too far ahead, he had no doubts Dreams could become a national brand. 'I actually imagined that the company would grow to even bigger than it is now. I wasn't doing it to just run one shop. A proper entrepreneur is never satisfied. I'm always thinking, "there's someone else in that rich list that's got more money, or someone that owns more stores". That's what gets me up in the morning.'

Dreams now delivers 6,000 beds every week, from its 100-strong fleet of vans. 'It's a necessary evil', says Mike who describes distribution as the company's biggest challenge. But ever the customer service enthusiast he can turn even his biggest hurdle into a way of making the company stand out.

If a Dreams driver delivers your bed in the rain, he'll put on a special pair of slippers to avoid leaving a messy trail. 'You've got to focus on customer service if you want repeat business', evangelises Mike. 'The slippers cost us virtually nothing but it's all the customers can talk about after they've had their bed delivered.'

The same rules apply to his attitude to staff. 'Recruiting and keeping good staff is hard but we find ways around those problems. The main thing is you can't skimp on salaries. It's worth paying 10% more for an employee that's twice as good.'

Despite his decision to sell, the future still looks bright for Dreams or, as Mike still calls it, his 'fifth child'. Sales during 2007 soared by 27% to just under £200m, with profit up 88% to £13.3m, with plans in place for a further 50 stores and franchising of the Dreams model overseas.

Mike is still involved with the company and is also mentoring for The Prince's Trust.

John Spooner

Experience: Former MD of Monsoon/Accessorize. Also worked for Liberty and Peter Jones.

John Spooner is best known for his lead role in establishing high street giant Monsoon. In 20 years with the company, he occupied several key management positions. In 16 years as managing director, John oversaw the company's most prolific growth period, as well as the emergence and expansion of sister brand Accessorize.

In 1998 he led the company to a £352m stock market flotation, before stepping down as MD in 2001 to become international director and take control of the group's roll-out overseas.

After exactly two decades at the company, he left in 2004.

John's first foray into retail came at department store Peter Jones in London's affluent Sloane Square where he answered a window ad for temporary Christmas staff after an argument with a disgruntled flatmate who was sick of him constantly stealing food. After liking it rather more than he anticipated, John joined permanently as a management trainee. However, within 18 months he followed one of his managers across the city to the West End and flagship department store, Liberty.

'I'd never planned to go into retailing', says John. 'My mother held a senior role in John Lewis but I'd always vowed I'd never do what she did. But I found I actually quite liked retailing; there were lots of good-looking girls around and I had a flat around the corner where I could roll out of bed at 8.59am.'

John held various positions at Liberty working in HR, training, and merchandising before rising to general manager and taking responsibility for setting up the company's regional operations. 'That was a wonderful period of my life. It was a company with strong family traditions and I got on well with the Stewart-Liberty family. But the world of cut and thrust beckoned and while I was at Liberty one of the concessions that I was responsible for was Monsoon.'

At the time a reasonably small business, John's then girlfriend and now wife had worked for the company and when John was offered a director's role it was too tempting to resist. 'I liked the culture. Monsoon was young and it had 100-odd staff, that was very different to the 1,000-plus working at Liberty. I felt it had great potential and would also give me the potential to earn some real wealth as a stakeholder in a business.'

After joining as retail director in just 18 months John was promoted to MD and charged with taking the company to the next level of development. 'The turnover was about £4m when I joined and when I left it had more than 450 outlets and revenues of over £270m.'

His first role was to introduce bigger company processes to what was still a small business set-up. 'On my first day, I asked to see the trading figures and was told I'd have to wait a day or so and the only way to do it was to phone around every shop myself. But from there a great empire grew, as they say'.

John also oversaw the emergence of sister company, Accessorize which opened its first store in Covent Garden the year John joined and, of course, has gone on to be a retail success story in its own right.

The growth of both Monsoon and Accessorize, certainly up to the point of flotation, was strictly organic and John's not a believer in unnecessary fundraising. 'We worked on the principle that the company expanded within its own abilities to generate cash. It didn't borrow money, in fact it never borrowed money. It was purely organic growth and while growth might have been limited by that rule, it was a strategy which I supported as it meant we weren't always running back to the bank or chasing a bank manager's expectations. We always tried to do what was right for long-term success of the business!'

After the flotation, John had a desire for change and while he waited until the time was right for the business, made the decision to relinquish the position of MD. 'I did miss it, but I was exhausted from living in London during the week while my family were in the countryside and I didn't really enjoy corporate life. I always found the public element, and all the politics and regulations that go with it, difficult to live with and work around. It was a process alien to my nature. We had a private business mentality'.

His role as international director was one John relished, particularly because it was project-based, part-time and enabled him to get back to working with young, entrepreneurial teams looking to find new ways to exploit emerging markets.

Since leaving Monsoon, John has been working with and mentoring a string of emerging retail companies in what he describes as 'pro-bono' work. 'I loved, and still do, the energy of young people. I've done a lot of things but not for financial gain. Companies approach me for advice and I help them as best I can. I think I am thought of as pretty blunt and straight forward, but people are under no obligation to listen to me and that's the beauty of working without a fee: you can say what you like even when it's not what people want to hear'.

While John advocates mentoring as a valuable tool for new retailers he believes there's a lot to be said from learning the hard way. 'You have to make your own mistakes, because that's what you learn from. Make decisions and if you get them wrong just be honest with yourself and others, say sorry if necessary, move on and don't do it again!'

Paul Mathers

Experience: Paul, along with wife Gail, established Wiltshire-based Sherston Post Office Stores in November 2004 and has grown it into a thriving hub serving the village's local community.

Husband and wife team Paul and Gail Mather purchased both a shop and the village's Post Office, which were formerly run as two separate businesses. It was their first business venture; Gail's background was in teaching and retail, Paul had 30 years' banking behind him.

'There came a point when our son had completed university and we could reflect on what we really wanted from life – the answer was to work together for ourselves,' says Paul. The shop was a perfect fit.

Paul and Gail purchased the buildings using money from the sale of their former property, £20,000 savings and 40% borrowing in the form of a mortgage. The Mathers also had to set aside £40,000 to combine the two businesses, but it's proved a great success. Turnover for shop sales for financial year ending November 2007 was £420,000, up 50% from the 2004 accounts of the previous owner, while Post Office trade increased by 25%.

Customer service and attention to detail is a core focus for Paul and Gail. 'Nothing is too much trouble and we try and offer a completely personalised service,' says Paul.

It's an approach which in addition to financial reward, has seen the shop crowned 'Wiltshire Life Village Shop of the Year 2008' and make the national finals for the Convenience Retail Awards' 'Best Unaffiliated Independent Store Award' for 2008. The couple have also made a point of working with the staff they inherited and among the nine part-timers and one full-time worker they employ, the company benefits from 80 years of experience in the business and its previous formats.

The business hasn't been without its problems however, with the Mathers experiencing several prolonged power cuts resulting each time in the throwing away of hundreds of pounds of frozen goods.

But the couple are very much focussed and while branching out with a chain of stores holds no appeal, they're ambitious and expanding the business as much as they can. In addition to offering many new spin-off services to their offering including obtaining an alcohol licence, they're now working on plans to relocate to a new site across the road.

Lance Prebble

Experience: Project manager for Pole Position Ltd, a multi-channel retail operation which opened its first shop on London's Regent Street in April 2008. Lance has previously run his own record shop and co-owns a Swiss watch manufacturer.

Lance Prebble has spent 2008 opening the Motorsport-themed retailer Pole Position's first shop on one of the busiest tourist destinations in the world, London's Regent Street.

The brand was initially used by Simon Gook for a cosmetics brand endorsed by Formula One driver David Coulthard and applied to a range of premium motor-themed watches supplied by Lance's other company. Gook licensed the brand to a specialist motor model memorabilia shop based in the Regent Street premises in 2006, but negotiated to takeover the premises at the start of 2008.

Pole Position inherited 1,000 sq ft of retail space over two floors and a supply chain with the licensed providers of replica motoring clothing, but has scaled the operation back to a core offering of replica clothing, leisurewear, signed prints, books and DVDs.

With limited resources and a prime location lease to finance, Lance has been tasked with developing an exportable business model with plans to open concessions in other stores and possibly franchise out across Europe.

'Pole Position is a brilliantly aspirational brand', says Lance. 'You hear it used all the time not just in association with motoring, but life in general. It epitomises that romantic nostalgia of fast cars and champagne-swigging, womanising racing drivers of old. We're selling leading brands such as Ferrari and McLaren and the profile of today's drivers such as Lewis Hamilton attracts interest in our brand.'

Lance sees the Pole Position shop as the showroom for a multi-channel operation, with equal focus on web sales and direct mail, where he has over 10 years' senior experience. 'The Regent Street address, while extortionate, gives us half a chance to build the brand, but this is very much an integrated, multi-channel operation.'

While Pole Position is a child among grown-ups compared to the other companies that make up our featured experts, the fact it's still going through the journey you're about to embark on makes it all the more prevalent. 'I haven't had a day off yet and I'm here until 11 o'clock every night', reveals Lance. 'But that's what you've got to do if you want to succeed. It won't happen on its own, while almost everything that can go wrong will go wrong.'

That said, sales continue to grow by the day and Pole Position's future, whilst tentative at this stage, looks healthy.

Clare Thommen

Experience: Co-founder of two-store luxury lingerie boutique Boudiche

Former accountants Clare Thommen and Fiona McLean have no regrets about giving up promising careers to start luxury Scottish lingerie company Boudiche. 'I earned a significant salary, had a company car, received a management bonus, a non-contributory pension and all that jazz', says Clare. 'But really, I was more interested in starting my business and working for myself.'

Inside three years Clare and Fiona are already onto their second boutique with a thriving web business and have taken a six-figure equity investment from an experienced retailer. They were finalists in last year's Startups Awards and beat established competitors Rigby & Peller and La Senza to the 2007 Drapers Awards for 'Best Lingerie Retailer'.

The decision to jack in finance isn't looking a foolish one then, with tales of outrageous PR stunts and drunken awards ceremony shenanigans gathering attendees for their 'men-only' nights. Perhaps these girls weren't cut out for a life of accounts anyway! Indeed, their business partnership was even sealed over a cocktail. A Lemongrass Martini, for the record. 'I'd had frustrating experiences shopping for lingerie and after having been fitted properly a year or two before, couldn't understand why there wasn't this trendy, cool, stylish place to go and buy it', says Clare. 'We were having a drink and joking where we'd like to be in five years. I said "I'd love to be running my own business", and so did she. I mentioned my crazy lingerie boutique idea and she'd had the same thought when travelling in Australia a couple of years before. It felt like fate and we working on the business plan 24 hours later.'

The process from concept to launch was somewhat slower, however. 'We did a lot of researching. It had to be a brand we created, not just another independent shop. Boudiche is about service, luxury and indulgence; with the customer leaving with a gorgeous tissue wrapped bag feeling fabulous.'

It also took a while to gather the start-up capital. As they were both under 30, they qualified for a £1,000 grant, while the Prince's Scottish Business Youth Trust lent them £5,000. This along with some savings and bank borrowing proved enough, although Clare hasn't yet got over the fact that the bank, of all their finance options, proved the least supportive. 'They'd only give us 60% of the cash we needed and then put silly restrictions on us like insisting Fiona stay working for the first six months of the business. Fiona didn't and we just didn't tell the bank – if she had, we wouldn't have a business now.'

Before you start

Who, why, what and where?

Y ou've got as far as deciding you'd like to run a shop but there's so much to consider before you even start putting a business plan together or suggesting the idea to friends and family.

You have to decide whether you're prepared for the long hours and the sacrifices you'll have to make. If you're determined to make your dream of running your own shop come true, we take you through the first steps to making your dream a reality. From getting experience in other retail businesses or advice from entrepreneurs, to choosing your business structure; from identifying the key selling points of your idea to conducting market research. After this chapter, you should have a pretty good idea of your concept, and whether it can work.

In this chapter we'll cover:

- Who's suited to running a shop
- The experience you need
- Support networks
- Business partners
- Market conditions
- USPs
- Identifying your customers
- Researching the market
- Testing your concept
- Choosing a location
- Buying an existing business

➡ WHO IS SUITED TO RUNNING A SHOP?

If you want it enough, then you're almost certainly suited to running your own shop and business. There are reams of studies, reports and research dissecting the DNA of successful business people. The significance of nationality, ethnicity, gender, age, education, class, experience, wealth, socio-political demographics, access to support and finance, and every other remotely explorable contributing factor have been analysed to death.

What conclusions have ever been drawn? None worth listening to, other than, in theory at least, there's not anyone, from any background and any walk of life, that can't successfully start and run their own business. So be assured, whatever your concerns and anxieties: you can do it.

'Doing it' is actually far more representative of the average entrepreneur's make-up than any of the numerous factors detailed above. People who start their own business are the ones who stop talking about their dreams and plans and actually make them happen.

They're the people that when everyone sits in the pub, office or park talking about what a great idea it would be to start a business doing this or that, are still thinking about it the morning after and for the rest of the week when everyone else's minds have moved on. They're the ones who scribble the idea down, keep turning it over in their head, getting more and more excited by every new angle that unfolds. Of course, they'll do this multiple times with multiple ideas, but one time they'll convince themselves it could actually work in real life and set about making it happen.

They take that big scary step out of the secure world of a guaranteed pay cheque for the risky life of running a small business. It rarely happens in one leap however, most people start exactly where you are now: researching what it's really like and the big exciting journey ahead.

Motivation

For surprisingly few, money is the main motivation. For others, being their own boss is the decision maker. For most it's to realise a dream, idea or desire to live a life that's more fulfilling, whether that be working closer to their family, in an environment they're more comfortable with or simply the challenge of earning their own income.

This is the most common reason people decide to open a shop. It's one of the most popular businesses for couples and families looking to spend more time together to start and one of the most accessible ways to work for yourself.

Others, such as those made redundant or those who, for whatever reason, struggle to find employment, turn to running their own businesses because they feel there's little alternative way to get ahead. But they still 'do it' instead of giving up. People start their own business for individual and deeply personal reasons and as such what's perceived as 'success' is almost always about personal challenges.

> **FROM THE EXPERTS:**
> ## Mike Clare, Dreams plc
>
> My father had his own business and my mother had her own shop where I spent a lot of time growing up and used to look after it. I always knew I wanted to go into retail.

What it takes

Enthusiasm and motivation aren't all it takes of course, as proved by the number of super-keen people who put every last drop of energy into starting businesses only to see them fail within the first year. That's obviously something we hope doesn't happen to you, but it could. Don't be put off by statistics though. Yes, people fail but many succeed as well, and remember, it's a personal measure. Lots of first-time business people don't succeed in others' eyes but use the experience positively to either start another business or return to employment with a greater sense of fulfilment.

That said, business is all about balancing risk and unless you ensure you're fully aware and prepared for how running a business will impact on your life, you're increasing your risk.

The realities of opening a shop

Becoming your own boss and setting up a small business is one of the most rewarding, exciting and fulfilling things you can do in life, but it's also one of the most stressful, testing and demanding experiences. It's often said getting married and moving house are the two most stressful events most people take on in life and starting a business should definitely be the third.

If you think you're escaping the '9 to 5' or 'the rat race' as often referred to in other business books, think again. Forget the idyllic movie representations of business people enjoying long lunches, days on the golf course or at the beauty spa. Unless you happen to strike it rich and come up with the next IKEA, that vision is nothing more than fictitious.

For at least the first two to three years, put the holidays on hold and expect to work longer and harder than you are now. Expect to make sacrifices with family and friends who, no matter how much you explain, won't understand why you've turned into an obsessed bore who ruins dinner parties and nights out with, literally, 'shop talk'. You'll need the emotional resilience to cope with feeling isolated from your usual support networks; and will need to find the time to find new ones while explaining while you've time to do this to all the people you're placing on hold.

IN MY EXPERIENCE:

Paul Mather, Sheraton Post Office Stores

You'll be working 75 hour weeks relentlessly. At first there is so much to do and learn. You soon learn there's so much more to do than simply serving the customers and it's so easy to fall behind.

For shop owners, the longer hours and isolation can be exaggerated. Sure you'll be mixing with the public, but your chance to get out and meet other business owners are limited during opening hours which are likely to be seven days a week. Holidays? No problem, providing you can afford and trust full time staff to open up, close, go to the bank for you, not mess up your supplier relationships and get up in the middle of the night if some idiot sets off your alarm.

TIP

Test number one: if this, instead of putting you off, is making you want to get started this very second, then you could have what it takes. Indeed, you could have the bug real bad.

Analysing your skills

It doesn't mean you're there yet though, and while passion and determination are compulsory assets for any entrepreneur, in excess they can be dangerous. Critical skills are important and none more so than when looking at yourself – and that starts now.

There are skills a business can't survive without. At its most naked your business needs you to have a basic understanding of accounting; an ability or inclination to sell; confidence in negotiation when acquiring; a natural inquisition for opportunity; decisiveness; leadership; initiative by the bucket load and, especially for running a shop, an firm understanding of the customer experience.

Essential skills

- The simplest understanding of accounts
- An aptitude for selling
- Negotiation skills
- Decisiveness
- Leadership
- Initiative
- The ability to multi-task
- Understand customers

There are heads of industry making billion pound decisions affecting hundreds of thousands of people who'll happily admit their skillsets don't stretch so far. Indeed, there's another industry making rich trade coaching and consulting business people and managers to recognise their skill gaps and bring in others to plug them.

That's where the reality of running a small business bites: you're highly unlikely to have that luxury from day one – maybe even day 356 or 752. Running a small business is a demanding, jack-of-all-trades challenge where you, and only you, will be at the centre of all activity. Sure, you can hire an accountant and a sales person but you'll the need the critical nous to read the progress of your business in a blink and that takes certain abilities and a rounded perspective.

It's these abilities that dictate who can run a business and who can't. The upside is that you can teach and equip yourself with the basics. If you want to succeed bad enough, you won't be embarrassed about admitting where you need to go back to school, ask questions and get help. You'll make mistakes, learn from them and move on. Remember, each time you do that and pick up something new the risk of failure decreases and chances of success grow.

Ultimately, if you have the desire; are realistic about what you're letting yourself in for; are willing to learn and get your hands dirty, there's certainly no reason why you can't succeed in business running a shop. That doesn't mean you will, of course, but there's only one way to find out!

> **FROM THE EXPERTS:**
> **John Spooner, Monsoon**
>
> The most common trait is actually passion. Yes it helps to understand finance but there are plenty of financially illiterate rich and successful people. Peter Simon who started Monsoon is slightly dyslexic and failed his exams, but he's done okay. If there are key attributes for succeeding in retail I'd say it's more likely to be people management skills.

Experience needed

Technically, you don't need any experience to run a shop. There's no reason you can't succeed without having previously worked in a shop. Certainly there are no regulations or license requirements related to the actual ownership or running of shops without experience to stop you, and many of the most successful retail brands littering our high streets were started by people who had no business or working retail experience at the point they first flicked the 'open' sign.

Statistically, there's no evidence that people are more likely to succeed if they've been in business before and the increasing numbers of 'teenpreneurs' making their fortunes fresh out of school proves a lack of experience certainly shouldn't be a barrier.

> **FROM THE EXPERTS:**
> **John Spooner, Monsoon**
>
> Experience can also work against you because you pick up another shop's prejudices and actually sometimes it's better to just make mistakes and learn from them.

It's also true you'll learn most from the mistakes you'll inevitably make. Just as you really learn how to drive only after you've passed your test, no amount of experience will prepare you for the many unexpected hazards and pitfalls you'll have to learn how to swerve once you're in the driver's seat.

> **FROM THE EXPERTS:**
> ## Mike Clare, Dreams plc
>
> It's better to have experience and ideally you should get some. It's free training; well, actually, you get paid for it!

It'd be foolish to discard the value of experience, however. Regardless of what anyone tells you, banks and investors operate on a purely risk against reward policy and the fact that they'd prefer a proven track record in business or industry over almost any other factor in an investment proposition should tell you everything you need to know about the importance of experience.

It might not be backed up statistically, but it's instinctive to trust someone with experience to do something well than someone just starting out. If you visit the dentist do you place your trust in the senior member of the practice or the latest recruit fresh out of college? There's no reason why the junior wouldn't have a wider knowledge of the latest practises and be the more skilled operator of course, but he or she would have it all to prove and that's the position you'll find yourself in if you go into business and running a shop cold without any experience.

It's also a fair assumption that the more experience you have, the better informed your decisions are. The more of the pitfalls you know about, the earlier you'll see them and the easier it'll be to avoid them. Founder of easyJet and the numerous easyGroup brands, Sir Stelios Haji-Innonou, is known as a risktaker, and while a supporter of young entrepreneurs, he believes 28 is a better age to start a business than straight from school or university because by then you'll have had time to understand how companies operate and, crucially, made mistakes at someone else's expense.

Identifying experience

In essence, this is fairly obvious. Knowledge is power etc. However, by the very fact you feel it necessary to pick up this book, I'm assuming you haven't previously started and run your own shop; or if you have, you haven't done it in a long while.

Possibly you've worked in retail. If you've worked in retail even at a shop floor level, you'll be feeling fairly confident you understand about the everyday operations of running a shop. If you've management level experience of ordering and maintaining stock, organising staff rotas, security, store layout, special offers etc, even better.

It might be that you've business experience. Maybe you've run a different business in the past or come from an accounting background so feel comfortable in business models and making the books balance, or it could be you're a champion sales or marketing person who thinks you're capable of sculpting a killer brand.

IN MY EXPERIENCE:
Paul Mathers, Sherston Post Office Stores

My wife, Gail, had worked for Marks & Spencers so had solid retail experience and from my working time vetting business plans in the bank I knew the critical issues that could impact on a business. That said, nothing prepares you for actually running a business.

It's often said, 'just because you've eaten in a lot of restaurants it doesn't mean you've any idea how to run one', and the same goes for shops. Be careful you don't fall into this trap. For instance, when you purchased the shoes you're now wearing it's highly unlikely you were thinking about what shifts the person serving you was on that week, how much they earned, what percentage of the store's income that was, how much the mark up on the shoes was, how many were left in stock, when the next delivery or range was due, whether the supplier agreement included instore marketing merchandise or other vagaries of running a business such as who lets the cleaners in and out at unsociable hours.

It's always different on the other side of the counter and no matter how much you think you already know, there will be more to learn. Alan Yau grew up in the restaurant industry and has gone on have great success with Wagamammas and restaurant Hakasan. However, he initially struggled with Wagamammas' promise to deliver food quickly in a less formal environment. The answer: get a job at Burger King to find out how the fast food world worked and what he could take from it.

> **TIP**
>
> The danger comes in assumption. Too many people think because they know retail inside out they know what it takes to run a retail business, and likewise just because you've run the finance function of a blue chip company it doesn't mean you've understanding of what sales techniques turn browsers into buyers.

Where possible your experience should be relevant to the type of shop you want to run. The operation of a newsagent differs greatly to that of a furniture shop. A newsagent will open early and close late in an area of busy passing trade or near transport links, selling goods delivered daily supplemented by supplies from a cash 'n' carry; while a furniture store is likely to open in more civilised hours in a retail location governed by ample parking and road access, relying heavily on marketing to draw customers and working with a small number of suppliers.

Florists, fishmongers and butchers start their days in the early hours at markets; some shops are more staff intensive than others; some attract loyal passionate employees, others by their very nature appeal to students and have a high turnover of staff.

So it can make sense to try and get experience in a shop environment similar to that you're looking to start in. However, behind all these different operations lies a retail model: all buy a product at one price and sell it on at another; hopefully making a profit after the various costs of operation are accounted for.

In this respect it's perfectly possible to learn how to run the accounts of selling home goods in an arts and crafts shop. In turn, it can actually be an advantage to have experienced diverse practises so you're able to apply a broader thinking to your strategic decisions, especially when looking to carve a niche or innovate in areas desperate for a new approach.

As I began by saying, you shouldn't be put off from opening a shop if you've never worked in retail. No matter what it says in the business manuals, if you've set your heart on starting-up and got as far as buying this book, you're highly unlikely to now put your grand plans on hold for a year or two while you enlist on a trainee management course at WH Smith.

Likewise you might have been working in retail all your life so how on earth do you go and land a job that teaches you how the business side of an operation works?

The reason a lot of you decide to plough on without experience contrary to those disapproving business advisors who seem to get more satisfaction from tutting and saying 'we told you so' when businesses go wrong, is more down to a lack of time or money than arrogance or naivety.

Haven't got any experience? Get some!

Most people know they should probably get some experience but aren't sure where to fit it in or even how to get the experience. If you're working full-time it's often unrealistic to expect you to get a job in a shop during the evenings, especially if you've a family. Likewise, once you've stopped working and sacrificed the security of a salary, getting a job in a shop for the sake of picking up some experience can easily seem time you can ill afford.

There's no one answer that'll work for everyone. For some people, getting a job in a shop on a weekend day while you serve out your notice of employment is the obvious solution; for others it's a case of dedicating a period of your pre-start-up or 'research' time to getting some inside information.

It might seem awkward to apply for a job you're not committed to or perhaps even over qualified for and it's not beyond comprehension you'll be asked about this. Here you have a straight choice: to come clean or lie. The choice is yours but you'd be surprised how many owner-managers will understand your situation and welcome the help of someone who's keen to learn, especially if you're able to offer them your services for free.

If you're really unable to commit a period of time to getting experience, ask a shop owner if you can shadow them for a typical day in the life of the business – or at least ask if you can buy them a meal or a drink in exchange for them imparting their wisdom.

Making these initial contacts might feel awkward and scary, especially if you're not accustomed to the world of business networking, but just remember, all the people you approach were once in your position. If you get a no – polite or otherwise – just brush it off and move on to someone else.

Support networks

The first support network you'll need is your family and friends, regardless of whether they're directly involved or not. No matter how hard you attempt to make sure it doesn't, starting and running a business will impact on your family, so it's essential you prepare them for what's ahead.

If your family (spouse, children, parents) aren't on board with you 100%, at some point you, your business, and/or your family will bear the consequences.

New businesses require a tremendous amount of time and nurturing to develop and become successful; time that is taken from elsewhere, often from the family. Unless you're starting a 'family' business where all members are participants, someone will inevitably feel left out, or neglected. Our family members don't always share the same dream we have. Their priorities may be something far from business success.

To make sure our families don't suffer due to our own ambitions, before you pursue your dream business, sit down with them and discuss the following:

● Will the business venture take away from quality time spent with family members? If so, how much is acceptable to all involved?
● Will the new business be initially funded or supported using family monies? If so, will this put a financial strain on the family?
● Do all family members agree this is a potentially successful business idea?
● Do all family members realise that most new businesses do not succeed?
● If the business is not showing signs of becoming successful, what operational time period will the family tolerate before the business is considered a failure and should be sold or closed down?
● If the new business fails, what is the alternative plan for income?

Some of the questions listed above may not have obvious answers until the business has started up and operated for some period of time. Since circumstances may vary regularly with new business, plan to review this list with the family about every six months to see what situations may have changed.

Your family needs to be in total support of your new business idea, or somewhere and at some point, somebody will suffer. Consider whether your 'big idea' is worth the possibility of distancing yourself from your loved ones, or even the finality of a possible divorce. Business owners with complete family support stand a much greater chance of success. Talk to your family and trust in their opinion.

Support from other entrepreneurs

The reason we asked some of the leading names in retail to contribute to this book is that there's simply no better place to get advice than from those that have, as the saying goes, 'been there, done it and got the t-shirt'. Entrepreneurs trust other entrepreneurs more than anyone else and naturally form support networks that might at first appear cliquey but are almost always actually born simply out of a shared understanding of each other's fairly unique lives.

Like all relationships you'll find that with support networks you'll get out what you put in. Networking comes naturally to some people; it fills others with dread. If you're the first sort of person, you're probably already aware of the value of getting out and meeting others. In business you can't know too many people (actually that's not true, there are networking addicts who spend so long swapping business cards, they forget there's an actual business to be run) or enough 'friends' to call on to get you out of a mess.

IN MY EXPERIENCE:
Paul Mathers, Sherston Post Office Stores

We liaise with other small shop keepers and owners of sub Post Offices. It allows you to get a different perspective on issues that may be bothering you and that can really help – it's good to talk!

If you're the second type of person, you're going to have to be brave and bite the bullet. Get yourself to a business networking event, have a glass of wine and simply chat to people about what you're doing. The likelihood is it won't be half as scary as you make it out to be in your mind and, remember, most people have been in the same boat as you.

TIP

Events like Startups Live, which you can find more detail on at www.startupslive.co.uk, will give you the opportunity to meet hundreds of other budding entrepreneurs and new business owners, some of whom will know the answers to the questions you're struggling to find answers to.

Retail is an industry where it pays to have contacts, be they simply peers to bounce ideas off, for mutual promotion or for advice on more complex issues that crop up such as planning permission – it always pays to have a mate at the council or an influential friend who's a lawyer, for instance.

Networking is also a great way of picking up recommendations. Most people recommend people they use – whether good or bad – so don't swallow their advice blindly, but knowing an accountant or lawyer who's experienced in your sector or knowledgeable of the area is a far more valuable lead than your standard Google search.

Don't confine your networking to physical events, either. Social networking is growing beyond the fun and games of Facebook and MySpace into a serious business tool and with sites such as LinkedIn, Smarta.com, BT Tradespace and Startups.co.uk you can interact with other entrepreneurs and business advisors – and, of course, while it lacks face-to-face personal touch it's far less scary!

Also see what business bodies and lobby groups are out there both for small business and retailers. The Federation of Small Businesses, Forum of Private Businesses, British Chambers of Commerce and Business Network International are all recognised lobby and small business groups who aim to represent, champion and advice small businesses, while you should also contact the British Retail Association.

List of lobby groups and support organisations

The Federation of Small Businesses: www.fsb.org.uk

Forum of Private Businesses: www.fpb.org

British Chambers of Commerce: www.britishchambers.org.uk

Business Network International: www.bni-europe.com/uk

Business Link: www.businesslink.gov.uk

Startups: www.startups.co.uk

As well as at Startups, the government's official support service Business Link can provide you with practical advice, and it's worth reading up as much as you can about the various aspects of starting a business you're most concerned about. There's a wealth of information out there so take advantage of it.

Mentors

Finally, think about getting a mentor. The government is set to announce a national mentoring service and there are several companies who provide matching services.

You don't have to follow this route, though. You also don't need a high profile celebrity entrepreneur mentor. Someone who's done what you wish to do should be your number one criteria. An experienced entrepreneur who you can turn to once every month or so to test out ideas on and gauge advice from will prove just, if not more, valuable.

Don't be scared to approach someone you don't know. Many entrepreneurs feel a responsibility to encourage and help others and will be only too willing to help. If they're not it'll almost certainly be because they're simply too busy (either running their own businesses still or possibly helping someone else). If that's the case, ask someone else. You'll soon get used to moving on quickly and without a grudge when met with the word 'no'!

IN MY EXPERIENCE:
Clare Thommen, Boudiche

We had a lovely mentor through the Prince's Scottish Youth Business Trust when we started and still keep in touch. Six months in we were then introduced a more high level retail mentor, Chris Tiso, CEO of Tiso's Ltd, an outdoor clothing and equipment specialise with 30 UK stores. His support and contacts gave us the confidence at time we desperately needed it and the bank weren't offering any help.

The more support you actively surround yourself with, the less likely you'll feel like you're in this on your own. For all the highs running your own shop will bring, there will be down times too and understanding from your family and friends, and knowledgeable contacts to seek advice from will be worth their weight in gold.

FROM THE EXPERTS:
Mike Clare, Dreams plc

People say go to the government support services but they're just retired bank managers who've never run a business. You're better off seeking a real entrepreneur and getting their advice.

➡ GOING INTO BUSINESS WITH PARTNERS/FRIENDS

Shops are one of the most popular family or couple-run businesses and, indeed, they can be great businesses to run with other people. After years of living separate working lives, couples often see a shop as a way of spending more time together. Likewise, who better to trust sharing such an enormous financial and emotional challenge with than your closest friends?

It's easy to see why, idealistically at least, it appeals. When you consider how much of our waking lives we spend earning money to enjoy in comparatively small spaces of time with the people that mean most to us, combining the two to get the best of both worlds is a compelling argument.

What's more, it can work brilliantly. The attributes for a healthy relationship – trust, honesty, the ability to listen, understanding, the unity of or tolerance of shared or different interests – translate well into business.

Clarifying responsibilities

Innocent Drinks was started by three friends who knew they'd simply like to start a business with each other and they tried several ideas, such as swipe card security for residential front doors and a bath filling timer device, before settling on smoothies. All three had different specialist areas and were confident they'd complement each other and get along well enough for the business to prosper.

Similarly, family businesses continue to prosper, especially where each member is clear about their responsibilities and relationship with each other within the business.

> IN MY EXPERIENCE:
> ## Clare Thommen, Boudiche
>
> Fiona and I have lots of fun and a really healthy competitive streak. We also have clear defined roles so add different things to the business.

Such clarity is the key to making a business started with friends or family work. It's essential to be sure that aside from your personal relationships, there's a business case for working together. Ideally your skill sets should complement each other so the business benefits from supporting two people – if it's unlikely you'd otherwise recruit this person alarm bells should be ringing.

What can go wrong

If your decision to work together does make business sense, there's no reason you shouldn't continue: just be aware of the consequences. If the business doesn't work out then relationships could turn sour and the trauma of losing a business could be doubled by also losing an otherwise lifelong friend or partner. Is the sharing of your finances and knowledge (which you could get elsewhere) worth the sacrifice? Ultimately it's your call, but be wary of rushing into something you could regret and agree how you'll communicate inevitable frustrations with each other to keep the relationship healthy.

Choosing a partner

If your business partner is more of an associate than a friend, you need to be clear in your mind that you trust and like this person sufficiently to share such an epic journey with them. It's likely you'll be working intensively with them for a number of years so you'll clearly need to get on. Indeed, if you're not friends with them, you probably want to consider why if it's anything other than not knowing them intimately enough – and if that's the case, perhaps you need to know them better.

Aside from having the skills you don't have and vice versa, look for a partner with whom you have a natural business chemistry with; someone who can enthuse you and whom you can inspire. Good partnerships, from business to sport and even entertainment, combine characters who together can create a greater sum total than their individual efforts and that's what you should aspire to build.

FROM THE EXPERTS:
Mike Clare, Dreams plc

If you're working with someone else there's a good chance you'll fall out. All the big names people admire, Branson, Sugar, Dunstone, they all did it on their own and I'm a big believer in that. It's fraught with problems. You'll never see eye-to-eye on everything and the very nature of entrepreneurship is making the decisions yourself.

You'll need to balance reward, responsibility and risk. Make sure you're clear what your goals are for the business on a shared and personal level, what you want in the short, medium and long term, be clear what your respective roles are and ensure you're each staking the same degree of risk. And, simple as it sounds, make sure you're happy and comfortable and have clear lines of communication for it to stay that way.

> ### ⚡ TIP
>
> Don't be tempted to go into business with someone simply because they've financial backing and you haven't, or because they've the great contacts you need. If a partnership doesn't have a natural foundation it won't work.

However, with all partnerships, expect the unexpected. Two in five marriages ending in divorce shouldn't dissuade you from getting hitched, but it should be enough of a warning to get legally binding shareholder agreements drawn up. This should cover what happens to the business and shares if any combination of unthinkable outcomes occur including, as morbid as it might seem, either of your deaths.

➡ MARKET CONDITIONS

It's likely you've heard a lot about the current economic downturn. Indeed, like all of us, you've probably felt the impact on your mortgage repayments, on food prices or at the petrol station. There's no denying that economically it's a difficult time and unlike previous dips, a quick resolution doesn't appear forthcoming.

Banks have cut lending options and it's certainly a tougher climate in which to raise funds for a business than, say, two years ago. This, of course, also impacts on what consumers have to spend, with banks pulling back consumer credit that had, according to some commentators, insulated retailers from economic instability.

Even before the economic outlook became bleaker, huge changes in the retail climate over the past 20 years had brought into the question the future of the traditional small independent retail shop.

> **FROM THE EXPERTS:**
> **Mike Clare, Dreams plc**
>
> Banks have shut up shop at the moment, but this sort of thing goes in cycles. Lending money is banks reason for existing; it's all they do, so it won't last forever.

Changes in the way we shop

The rise of retail parks, out-of-town shopping centres, diversification of supermarkets across competing sectors and swallowing up of high street retail units by bars, restaurants, coffee shops and larger brand retailers are all seen as suffocating for independent retailers.

One of the major causes of this has been the rising cost of prime retail property. Larger multiple brands are able to secure long term rental deals based on turnover, while small businesses find themselves unable to compete and are restricted by upward only rent reviews. As more small shops are squeezed out of the high streets, increasingly it's only established brands that are able to take these plots.

Increased pedestrianisation of town centres, changes to planning and transport constraints and rises in parking costs have also made out of town shopping centres powerful propositions to consumers and contributed to declines in town centre footfall and a decentralisation of retail outlets.

The growing burden of regulation has also posed a competitive challenge to smaller traders. Research by small retailers' organisations suggests that regulation is an important influence on the profitability and longevity of their businesses.

The return of the independent shop

It was with some relief then that the British Retail Consortium released research insisting the future of small independent shops is nowhere near as grim as it might at first appear.

Contrary to popular belief the number of traditional retail businesses – greengrocers, bakers, butchers, fishmongers and a range of specialist shops – trading in the grocery sector across the UK has actually gone up in recent years. In 2005 there were 43,800. By 2007 that figure had grown to 51,700.

David Cameron has also announced proposals for substantial tax relief for small shops under a Conservative government while Mayor of London Boris Johnson has pledged to use section 109 of the Town and Country Planning Law to ensure developers reserve more affordable rents for smaller independent retailers.

Positive aspects

There are still plenty of reasons to be cheerful about starting a shop. The consumer might be spending less, but they're still spending. Indeed, budget store Primark saw first quarter sales for 2008 soar to £890m propelling it into 2nd place in behind M&S as the UK's favourite clothing brand.

OK so you're not about to start competing with Primark but its success does tell us about the market. Shops offering premium or strongly differentiated niches are prospering along with those providing discounted or budget prices. It is shops in the middle ground that are suffering. Former Tatler editor Jane Proctor recently said: 'It's either Prada or Primark, anything in between is a waste of money'.

Starting in a downturn can also be a positive. As hardnosed as it sounds, other businesses failing frees up retail units, keep leases low and floods the recruitment market with talented staff you otherwise mightn't be able to afford or attract.

If you can establish yourself on limited resources and build a loyal customer base when times are tight, you'll flourish in more affluent climates. There's never a bad time to start a good business, so don't let market conditions put you off: just make sure you plan even harder to get your offering spot on.

✦ TIP

There's no doubting it's a difficult time for retail but every company that fails presents a new opportunity and there's no bad time to start a good business. And if you can establish your model during a downturn, chances are it'll flourish when the economic climate improves.

➡ YOUR BIG IDEA – USPS (unique selling points)

You'll probably already know what type of shop you'd like to start and run. Indeed, when you first stumbled upon the idea of opening a shop, you were almost certainly thinking of running a certain type of shop.

For many of you it'll be as simple as wanting to run the type of shop you've always enjoyed shopping in. For others among you, a shop will represent an opportunity to spend your working day embracing a passion or hobby, such as antiques or music. The more opportunistic and entrepreneurial among you will have spotted a trend, gap in the market or need for a certain type of shop.

Even those of you who initially wanted to just run any shop are unlikely to have stopped your imagination skipping ahead of itself dreaming about what type of shop would suit you best. Essentially then, however unpolished, you'll have an idea of the type of shop you want to run; ie what your shop will sell.

Picking a type of shop is only half the challenge, though. Next you'll need to explore the specifics of that type of shop to start sculpting exactly what your offering to the market will be.

✦ TIP

Start by making a list of what will make your shop unique. Your USPs (Unique Selling Points) will define how your shop is different from the competition and will slowly build its identity and brand. Your USPs will be your sales story to convince people they should buy from your shop instead of elsewhere.

It's not enough to say you want to start a 'clothes shop'. For instance, let's revert to the Prada and Primark example of contrasting brands essentially both selling clothing. Both are extremely successful businesses and established brands, one sells dresses retailing in the thousands, the other for under a fiver. From price to target customer and premises, they're entirely different businesses making even the loosest shared label of 'clothing' all but redundant. Indeed, Ferrari is more closely aligned to Prada and ASDA to Primark.

IN MY EXPERIENCE:

Clare Thommen, Boudiche

It had to be a brand we created, not just another independent shop. Boudiche is about service, luxury and indulgence. Leaving with a gorgeous tissue-wrapped bag feeling fabulous.

The good news is, as a small business, you've far more flexibility and opportunity to find unique routes to appeal to customers. For example, it could be that you decide to sell exactly the same laptops as available in PC World or Dixons but also offer free delivery, installation of software and a beginner's tutoring service, so specifically appealing to elder shoppers or those less technically confident. It could even be as simple as focussing on just selling laptops and absolutely nothing else in a budget 'no frills' offering.

Your USP could be that you sell a wider variety of a niche product than any other store. Before Lush starting selling nothing but soap, that type of shop simply didn't exist for instance. Alternatively, one of Majestic Wine's initial USPs was that it only sold wine by the box load and took units with ample parking.

When drawing up your USPs, consider the following suggestions to differentiate your offering:

- Superior customer service
- No frills
- A wider or more focussed selection of products
- Premium
- Budget offering
- Child care facilities
- Faster, more flexible delivery
- Ethically sourced
- Environmentally friendly
- Better after sales support

> **FROM THE EXPERTS:**
> ## Mike Clare, Dreams plc
>
> It's important to be different. If it's not a unique idea, you can either provide better service, offer lots of stock or the best price. Price is very difficult, however, because you're usually buying at the same price so it's difficult to make a margin. But don't be afraid to copy either, if someone's spent years perfecting a model, why change it?

➡ WHO ARE YOUR CUSTOMERS?

Once you've a clear idea of what your shop will sell and what its USPs are, you need to define who your customers will be. Without doing this you won't be able to properly plot the viability of your idea in a business plan.

> **IN MY EXPERIENCE:**
> ## Paul Mathers, Sherston Post Office Stores
>
> Our key strength was being local to the village so we concentrated on what a supermarket couldn't provide. We knew we couldn't beat Tesco on price but we could offer unrivalled personal service, a friendly atmosphere and those little touches that people value.

To assess if your shop would work as a business you'll need to prove there are enough people in the area you're based who want the product you're selling for the price you're charging.

For some shops reliant on tourism or affected by seasonal peaks and troughs this can be a complicated process and will involve looking at visitor levels as well as regional populations; calculating varying incomes against monthly and annual overheads.

> ### ✦ TIP
> There are sure to be many more USPs to differentiate your business. Don't try and add them for the sake of it, but ensure your business is clearly defined from what's already out there and you have a firm idea of what your shop will offer.

Don't fall for the mistake of convincing yourself that just because you love the idea, then others will. Too many people skip the process believing 'if you build it, they will come'. It's a saying built in Hollywood not the real world, where the reality is people can't come if they don't exist . . . or they can't afford your prices . . . or there's a shop doing the same closer to where they live.

Unfortunately there are plenty of great sounding 'ideas' that simply aren't viable. Banks will expect to see evidence of an existing customer base and so should you if you're using your own money or, quite simply, you want the business to have a chance of working.

Identifying who your customers are

Before you can explore if your customer exists in sufficient numbers you need to establish exactly who you're looking for. There are standard demographic outlines of consumers you should use.

Social grade	Social status	Occupation	Annual earnings estimate
A	upper middle class	higher managerial, administrative or professional	£50k +
B	middle class	intermediate managerial, administrative or professional	£35-£50k
C1	lower middle class	supervisory or clerical, junior managerial, administrative or professional	£25-£35k
C2	skilled working class	skilled manual workers	£15-£25k
D	working class	semi and unskilled manual workers	£7-£15k
E	those at lowest level of subsistence	state pensioners or widows (no other earner), casual or lowest grade workers	£5-£7k

Lance Prebble, Pole Position

Our brand is aspirational, but our target customers probably aren't As or Bs, more likely C1s and C2s so we have to offer a combination of aspirational stock and affordable offerings that both gets people through the door and spending.

You essentially want to know what the profile of your target customer is: are they male or female, how old are they? What's their disposable income? What other brands do they also consume? How much would they spend with you and how frequently?

Research the market

Now you know what type of shop you want to start and who you'd ideally like your prime customers to be, you need to know if those people actually exist. Not only must they exist, they must exist where you can find and afford a shop.

One of the best places to start is by getting hold of a copy of your area's latest census, either online (from your local government website) or from your local library. Even better, get hold of censuses for several of the areas you could feasibly operate in so you can make direct comparisons – even if you're stuck on one location, having stats proving its suitability can make a compelling case to the bank so is still worth doing.

Paul Mathers, Sherston Post Office Stores

We made five different visits to the village at different times, watching people go in and out and to check how rowdy the pub was at closing time. We visited all the shops in the area as mystery shoppers as well as endless research on the internet.

The census should show you the population of the area; percentage of home ownership; percentage of people economically active (employed); the percentage of those retired;

Additionally there are several websites available that provide regional demographic information, such as www.upmystreet.com.

Consult retail statistics released by associations to identify trends in the type of shop you're looking to start and look for breakdowns by region. They'll also tell you retail footfall figures for streets you're able to afford property on and provide examples of the average revenues per square foot or per 1,000 people which you can use as a benchmark for estimating the size of your potential customer base.

Business Link and The British Library Business & IP Centre can also give you access to market reports and data that would cost thousands of pounds to buy copies of yourself.

Useful websites

Business Link: www.businesslink.gov.uk
The British Library: www.bl.uk

Homemade surveys

Carry out your own research with the public as well. Take to the streets and carry out surveys and questionnaires exploring anything that can prove your case that a market for your shop exists. Ask respondents how much they'd spend a month on the products you're planning to sell, how far they usually have to travel for those goods and ask them to tick if your USPs would make a difference to where they shopped.

Asking personal questions such as people's income or age is likely to put them off from taking part, so instead ask them to tick ranges which will fit with the demographic research you've unearthed and have identified as your target customer. The more people you interview within these ranges, the more powerful your research will be.

DIY market research

Questions to ask members of the public in your chosen location

- How often do you go into XX shops? – Hardly ever, once or twice a month, once or twice a week, more than twice a week
- How old are you – under 18, 18–24, 25–34, 35–50, 50+
- What's your wage bracket – Under £15,000, £15–20,000, 20–30,000, 30–50,000, 50–100,000, £100,000+
- Would you welcome a shop selling [enter your products here]

Research companies

There are professional research companies that you can hire to carry out feasibility studies. For most of you their services will be out of your price range and be wary of companies who claim to do this for comparatively low rates as it's likely they'll merely accumulate information already in the public domain that you could do for yourself.

Well carried out professional research can prove worth the investment however, especially if you're seeking substantial finance. If you pursue this route, be clear exactly what you're looking to achieve and perhaps even research investors first about how you can meet their expectations. And be careful what you spend. While some investors will be impressed by professional research, others will question your business acumen if you've spent a considerable slice of your start-up capital just proving a market exists.

TIP

Try the Research Buyers Guide when looking for reputable sources for market research. www.rbg.org.uk has a fully searchable directory of market research providers.

> **FROM THE EXPERTS:**
> ## Mike Clare, Dreams plc
>
> Don't pay anyone to do research for you. They'll own let it out to a load of housewives anyway. Do it yourself. Sit on a bench and study who walks past. You can tell if the people walking past have got money or the shops in the same row are doing well within minutes and from gut feeling. You can pay for it, but why bother? All the censuses are too out of date anyway.

➡ COMPETITION

Competition tends to come in two forms: directly from other shops in your area selling the same or similar products, and indirectly from other ways those customers can spend money they'd otherwise spend with you.

Direct competition is relatively simple to research and observe, but indirect competition is subject to constant change, market forces and trends. For instance, mobile phones have changed the spending priorities of teenage girls. Where once, their pocket money would be spent on cosmetics and clothing, a significant percentage now goes on top-up cards.

DVD rental shops don't just compete with other shops selling DVDs but also cinemas and online film websites, as another example. So it's not just rival shops you need to consider when looking at competition, but anything competing for a slice of your target customer's disposable income.

> **FROM THE EXPERTS:**
> ## John Spooner, Monsoon
>
> I've never spent too long looking at the competition or over my shoulder, it's better to concentrate on staying ahead of the game yourself.

Competition isn't always a negative however, and is increasingly seen as collaborative. Restaurants and estate agents have for years prospered by clustering together and the successful rise of retail parks full of rival retailers is proof it can often pay to be located alongside competitors.

Indeed, a highly successful shop in an area could suggest there's room for another, especially if customer service and satisfaction has suffered as a result of it being overworked. For instance one Southeast town is the home to two church supplies shops sitting happily across the street from each other. Competition then should be seen as an opportunity to prove the case for your business as well as a reason for disproving it.

Researching and learning from competitors

That said, no matter how much you've set your heart on running a certain type of business in your hometown and are convinced you'd do it better than the incumbents, it rarely makes sense to open a new shop in a saturated market. Remember, you're proving the market as much your shop.

As frustrating as it might seem, people don't always shop with their heads and even if you present a better product for a superior price, some shoppers simply won't break habit or misplaced loyalty so it's unlikely you'd ever take 100% of another business' customer base.

TIP

If you're feeling especially brave, go and speak to the owners. Be honest and say you're thinking of starting a shop in the area, ask them for tips and advice. You'll find many are surprisingly helpful and the ones that aren't, well you won't be any worse off, and you'll know more about the kind of people you're up against.

You should cross reference the number of competitors in your area, and their USPs, with your demographics in order to establish if there's room for another business. It could be that on reflection you identify a new USP that would give you a better chance of securing market share – and that's perfectly healthy. This process is all about proving the business viable so don't be scared to tweak the concept where sensible.

Competitors should also provide a way of benchmarking your proposition and pricing. Visit them, take in the customer experience, where possible speak to customers to get a feel for their reputation and try to identify as many places as possible where you can score an advantage.

➡ HOW TO TEST YOUR CONCEPT

Take every opportunity you can to test your concept. It's likely you'll still be tweaking it a year into opening but by then you'll have all the overheads, time constraints and running responsibilities to deal with, so take every chance you get while researching and starting-up to test, test and then test again.

Visit markets, fairs, fêtes, car boot sales anywhere you've a captive audience to sell to or get feedback. To test if people like your products, give them away in exchange for honest feedback – and that doesn't mean to friends and family whose opinion is always biased no matter how much they insist they're being truthful.

It's important to try and sell as well. You'll quickly find out if your prices are too high, or on the flipside, if you're shifting units like hotcakes, then perhaps you're not charging enough.

Try selling online

eBay's global reach might have proved itself a rival to several types of small shop but it's your friend when it comes to testing your concept, as well as research. Indeed, many shops now start by selling online through eBay – before they even have premises.

However, you need to veer on the side of caution here even if you're selling good numbers through eBay. Remember, people buy online in very different ways and your success won't necessarily be converted to a shop. Moreover, your business model selling on eBay won't incorporate any of the overheads a physical location will bring – that's the reason so many shops have gone out of business as a result of online competition. Be careful to factor this into your analysis.

Feedback

For any concept testing you do, make sure you record the results, from eBay sales, or units sold at a market, to anecdotal customer feedback – it's all good for tweaking your model and also compelling evidence to use in your business plan and when pitching for finance; even for PR.

The founders of Innocent Drinks constantly refer to the day they tested a selection of initial smoothie recipes out on visitors to a jazz festival asking people to place their empty cups in either a 'yes' or 'no' bin under the banner 'Should we quit our jobs to make these smoothies full-time?'.

The more feedback you can get, the closer you'll be to selling products people actually want once you're open and hopefully you'll be building customer and brand awareness along the way.

> **IN MY EXPERIENCE:**
> ## Clare Thommen, Boudiche
>
> We did a lot of email surveying but also took to the streets to find out where people bought their lingerie from at the time, what brands they preferred and where they would prefer a new store to be located.

➡ CHOOSING THE RIGHT LOCATION

Ever wondered why newsagents tend to be located outside bus stops, stations and near schools? Consider why sometimes you'll stop at different convenience stores dependent on whether you're driving or walking; why real specialist niche stores seem to survive in obscure, tucked away locations with little passing trade, or why furniture stores, DIY shops and garden centres tend to cluster together with ample parking and loading space.

> **IN MY EXPERIENCE:**
>
> ## Paul Mathers, Sherston Post Office Stores
>
> We were very clear what we wanted. Site was paramount. If it wasn't at the heart of the village or needed a sign for people to find it, we discarded it.

None of these are accidents and where your shop is located will play a major part in how successful it is. By now you should have proven there's a significant volume of customers in the town or city you're looking to open your shop, but that's only half the battle. Unfortunately, even the perfect product at the best price won't guarantee sufficient visitors unless you find a location that makes it convenient to get people through the doors.

Most shops rely on passing trade, however it's likely you'll have to work harder than simply looking for a site with the densest passing population. The likelihood is those sites have already been snaffled up by the big brands and are usually out of a start-ups price range.

> **IN MY EXPERIENCE:**
>
> ## Lance Prebble, Pole Position
>
> We're on one of the busiest tourist streets in the world, which gives us a fighting chance. But then again, footfall means nothing if people don't come through the door.

As we'll repeat endless times in this book and should possibly become a mantra you constantly refer back to, start by looking at the customer. Who are they and how do they behave? Target sites that will make you a convenient choice for them.

What to look for and what to avoid

If parking is important to your customers and you're selling cumbersome products you'll need access to car parks (if free even better) or possibly an out of town shopping centre. If your target customers are young people, consider locality to schools, colleges, universities and other facilities enjoying good use. If you're looking to start a convenience store or newsagents, look for locations next to local amenities and away from supermarkets.

Be wary of the higher floors of shopping centres which almost always see less trade; locations where new retail parks or shopping centres have opened and are likely to pull away trade; where there's a high turnover of businesses; areas around planned redevelopment and road changes. Don't be blinded by appealing sites that simply don't get the passing trade you'll need.

The local council might also be able to provide local footfall figures, detailing walk through populations by street. Market research companies will also sell you this, but it's something you can also measure yourself. If you do, be careful to take samples at different times of the day taking into account traditional periods of influential activity such as rush hours, lunch times, after pub closing etc.

It's also worth speaking to your local council or regional development agency to see if there are any incentives, grants or tax breaks for opening your shop in a certain area – or even relocating to a different city. It might not be what you had planned, but free rent and a support grant could make all the difference to your business' survival.

➡ BUYING AN EXISTING BUSINESS

You don't have to start from scratch and shops are one of the most popular businesses to buy. There are many reasons to buy a shop instead of setting one up. As well as premises, you'll be acquiring a ready made proposition and customer base. It'll certainly take less time than starting up yourself and if you buy a healthy, profitable shop it'll almost certainly be cheaper as well as more likely to survive than a new business.

The challenge is finding a business to buy that is 'healthy and profitable' and doesn't just have the potential to be. Or worse still, has no chance of fulfilling its potential. What you won't ever see is a sales blurb telling you this. It'll be up to you to distinguish what's worth buying and what's not and it's a notorious minefield.

Some of the world's top entrepreneurs and retailers have been lured by a bargain convinced they'll be able to sprinkle their magic dust and turn a profit – but have failed. For the first time buyer, buying a business is riddled with risk but then so is starting up.

Do your research

If you decide to buy a shop, do as much homework as you can in a bid to limit that risk. Time is often limited but the more information you can find out about exactly what you're buying the better informed you'll be about the price you should be paying and exactly what you're letting yourself in for.

Make sure you speak to people. Ideally you'll want to speak to the sellers. If you're buying direct this won't be a problem but be wary of sellers who are reluctant to divulge too much information or open up the books; you can be sure there's a reason why. If you're buying through an agency who's reluctant for you to speak to the seller directly this is also be a warning sign. A good seller will be open about their reasons for selling, although it's fair to assume someone will be more forthcoming about wanting to retire or move away than dwindling sales – but you should be able to see this from their books.

Speaking to the owners will also help you establish if it's worth paying for 'goodwill', where you pay a premium in exchange for existing client contacts and customer information.

Speak to customers (if the sellers are happy for you to do this, it's a good sign); customers visiting competitors (ask them why they're not shopping at the place you're looking to buy and what would make them change their mind); and chat to suppliers to establish how relationships have been left and to suss out any bad debts.

> ### TIP
> Get an accountant involved. They be able to check the books for anything concerning or unscrupulous and will also advise you on the most tax efficient way to structure the purchase.

Make sure you speak to staff, as well. If you take over you'll be expected to honour their contracts under the TUPE regulations but just as importantly, they'll know the business better than you will. Keeping them on board, at least until you've found your feet, is likely to make sense and be good for continuity.

Once you've made a purchase, it's likely you'll still want to stamp your authority on the business. Certainly you'll need to be just as clear in your offering as if you were starting from fresh. The rest of this book is about starting a shop, but all the principles covered are just as relevant to the first time shop owner who's acquired a business as to those who have started their own.

Things to remember:

- It's too much hard work to start if you're not fully committed to seeing it through. Know what you're getting into before you start.

- If you don't have enough experience, get some before you open.

- Talk it through with friends and family. They may still offer support even if they're not convinced by the idea.

- If you can't do it alone, think long and hard about the type of person you want as a partner.

- Identify a USP from the very beginning.

- Do your research, and make it thorough.

- Know your competition inside out.

- Don't rule out the possibility of buying and adding to an existing business.

Planning

W e've made business plans the first priority in this section of the book because the hope is by the end of the chapter you'll have a damn fine one packed with detailed evidence of why your shop will succeed making a handsome profit and, if you need it to, wow the pants off a bank manager or investor.

We lay out all the information a good plan needs to include and how this will help you not only to secure funding for your venture but also equip you with a clear vision of how you are going to run your shop both now and in the future. It may be boring now, but by including details of your pricing strategy, your expenses, your predicted revenue and financial records you'll be left with a business plan which will be a useful tool you can adapt and refer to as your business plans progress.

In this chapter we'll cover:

- Writing your business plan
- Setting prices
- Budgeting
- Revenue forecasts
- Financial sheets

➡ BUSINESS PLANS

Now comes the tricky part. You've got a whole chapter and tonnes of researching and work to do before you get to that point – you didn't expect it to be that easy, did you? Here we'll talk about what your business plan actually needs to have. What it needs to look like, what it should prove, and the crucial information it needs to contain. You won't be able to actually write it yet, though. For that you'll need to compile all the data the rest of this section covers.

Don't be put off by writing a business plan. It's not difficult and if you do it properly it won't be tedious either. It should be a labour of love and every bit as exciting as the initial idea generating the enthusiasm that led you to pick up this book. Writing a business plan should further feed that enthusiasm. Why? Because by the end of the process you should feel you're able to transcend from idea to business; dream to reality. What's more you should have a document for others to believe you too.

Certainly, there's no avoiding writing a business plan; and the more you embrace it the more you're likely to actually find it a meaningful and useful process than merely a way of appeasing the bank. A good business plan will give you something to constantly refer back to when making tough decisions and strategy calls, and should be a working document you update as the business progresses.

FROM THE EXPERTS:
John Spooner, Monsoon

Have I done them? Yes. Am I a fan of them? No. They're good for critiquing and making you think what you're doing and you'll certainly need one if you're going to the bank with your begging bowl.

Writing a business plan

Before you start putting a plan together try and get hold of some examples from the internet or even by asking your bank what sort of document they expect to see.

Clare Thommen, Boudiche

Our first business plan was the best one and pretty much said it all. It was a side of A4 and we did it in the pub the night after we had the idea. It was more a 'mind map' we drew out with 'boutique' in the middle with spider arms and legs of how we'd market it, our target customer, ideal location, brands etc.

Don't worry too much about the design and layout of a business plan at this stage, though. Much like CVs, people often obsess unnecessarily about the supposed best format, structure, length and lay-out when what's far more important is that the document contains all the necessary information and is easy to understand.

What to include

Start by identifying and gathering the basic information you'll need.

A standard business plan outlines the following:

- What your business (your shop) will do
- Who your customers will be
- Why people will buy your products
- Evidence this market exists and its potential
- Evidence of why your business will survive when others don't; analysis of the competition
- Who you are and why you're going into business
- Why you believe you've got the skills and expertise to run a shop; your qualifications and experience
- Details of any other directors or key management
- How you will fund the setting up of the business
- How you will repay any money you borrow
- What your ongoing costs and overheads will be
- Sales and revenue forecasts for the first 12 months of business
- Details of suppliers and contracts
- Your goals for the first 12 months and then beyond that

That might sound fairly exhaustive, but it should be. Your business plan should present a watertight argument of why and how your shop will work. If it's not, then you should be asking yourself if it's still such a great idea. Consequently, be honest. Don't

> ### TIP
> Use your business plan to prove to yourself that your shop can survive and prosper, not just as a tool to accessing finance.

exaggerate revenues and underplay overheads in order to make the plan work. Bank managers will have seen thousands of applications in their time and will see straight through it – and, of course, you'll be kidding yourself and invalidating your business plan as a useful document. If anything, veer on the side of caution.

Many entrepreneurs I've asked say that with the benefit of hindsight when planning a business you should halve the income you anticipate and double the expenses you expect to pay – any discrepancy in your favour will be a bonus. Others I've interviewed insist they would never have secured the funding they needed without a few white lies and that whatever you ask for the bank will give you 20% less. Ultimately it's your call, but remember your business plan should plot your progress and skewing it for any purpose limits how much it can help you.

Keep it simple and don't try and write reams – an overly long verbose plan will irritate more than it impresses and investors will be far more concerned with being able to access concise key information than they will your poetic flair or pretty paper; it's a business plan not a year 9 school project. Where appropriate use bullet points and break up the text; bitesize chunks of information are far easier to absorb. Don't leave anything out but keep it brief; people can always contact you if they need to know more.

Now before you start, read on to see what you need to know to make the ultimate business plan for starting a shop.

> ### FROM THE EXPERTS:
> ## Mike Clare, Dreams plc
>
> You need a business plan but some people spend far too long writing it, researching it, tweaking it and never get around to actually starting. I say JFDI, Just Fucking Do It! The best business plan in the world won't account for things that happen outside your control so you might as well just get on with it.

➡ SETTING YOUR PRICES

Before you can plan anything, make any forecasts, plot any projections or arrive at a principle sum you'll need to borrow to start your shop, you need to think about roughly how much money you can make from the products you intend to sell. As it's difficult to tell exactly how much you'll sell, it's safer to start by looking how much profit you can make per item sold, often referred to as per unit. To do this, you'll need to start setting prices.

Exactly how much you intend to sell individual items for might seem like minutiae that can wait until later when you've 'big vision' considerations such as securing a bank loan, finding premises and creating a brand etc. However, it's actually a much bigger factor in deciding whether your business will work than any of those, and as such needs to be at the forefront of your planning. You can't possibly know how feasible a business is without being clear about the fundamentals of any retail operation: ie how much money you make per transaction.

The two key elements of deciding your price with be:

1. The costs of goods
2. Your operational expenses

The cost of goods should include any associated cost in the development or acquiring process such as packaging and delivery etc. Operational expense incorporates all your overheads rent, staff wages, marketing, technology etc.

The sum of the two costs subtracted from the price you set will, in theory, be the profit you generate – although, of course, there are many outside influences that have the potential impact on your bottom line.

You'll need to begin then by ensuring you know exactly how much your product costs to the point it goes through the till. You'll also need to establish the running costs of your business. You probably don't know all of them at the moment so make estimations and keep tweaking and adjusting the calculation when you know more.

When the likes of Peter Jones and Duncan Bannatyne berate budding entrepreneurs on Dragons' Den for not 'knowing their figures' this is exactly what they're talking about – and they're right as well. For your shop to succeed as a business, which is exactly what it is, you'll need to know at all points what any item you sell costs you to buy and how much you make when you sell it.

Otherwise you cease to be running a business, the aim of which remember, up and above all the lifestyle benefits it brings you, is to make money. It's that profit that will pay your salaries, mortgage and holidays (if you're lucky!) and what the bank manager or an investor needs to be confident of if they are to lend you money.

Developing a pricing strategy

Knowing what a product costs you and the percentage profit you'd like to make is rarely all it takes to make your shop's proposition viable, unfortunately. The missing key consideration in this equation is, of course, a customer base that wants to buy at this golden figure you've got sitting on your calculator!

For some products such as official sports merchandise or branded items like iPods the manufacturer will have a suggested or minimum pricing policy to avoid price wars or heavy discounting which, while making things easier, will limit ability to make the profits you've factored for.

Think carefully about setting up a shop stocking such goods as it's likely you'll be competing against large retailers who have the advantage of buying in bulk and multi million pound marketing budgets. If price was one of your USPs it's unlikely you'll compete here.

Competitive pricing

If you do decide to price below your competitors you'll need to work on keeping your overheads rock bottom. In the current economic climate, consumers are happy to shop around for the best price and may be prepared to sacrifice other aspects of their shopping experience to get them.

For instance, let's say you decide to try and undercut a shop selling premium home electronics. Unless you negotiate a superior supply rate with manufacturers, which is highly unlikely, then you'll need to find another way of reducing your overheads. So instead of a fancy showroom, free delivery, instillation service and warranty you offer a no frills discounted service.

Budget or no frills shops make some of the most profitable retail operations, but it's a strategy not without risk. Squeezing profits means there's little margin for error and you'll feel the impact of a drop in sales far quicker. Larger chains will know this and if they see you as a threat, could match your prices (even if meant they'd be selling at cost value or even a loss) to force you out of business.

> **FROM THE EXPERTS:**
> ## Mike Clare, Dreams plc
>
> It's difficult to compete on price because you're usually buying at the same price as competitors, so there's little room to cut a margin.

This is exactly how so many small shops went out of business at the point when large chains and supermarkets began to expand the diversity of their product ranges. Small shops already struggling to compete on cost simply had no room to manoeuvre or compete.

It's probably why there's been a rise in smaller shops looking to deploy prestige pricing models, charging more goods on the basis they offer something extra, be it location, better customer service or a unique twist. This is nothing new, of course, as the Great British grocery store or corner shop, has for years charged a small premium on most products for the convenience of being a few paces away.

> **IN MY EXPERIENCE:**
> ## Clare Thommen, Boudiche
> You've always got to provide value, but our brand isn't about being the cheapest. It's about luxury, quality fit and service in luxurious surroundings.

Business manuals will talk about a few other strategies for pricing:

Keystone pricing

This refers to the practice of simply doubling the cost price of a product, but it's fairly academic now as there are few products which offer the chance to make such a mark up.

Multiple pricing

This is an increasingly popular strategy and a clever way to incentivise shoppers into buying more than they originally intended, or to shift poor selling stock. It involves offering multiple products grouped together for one superior price. For instance, two pairs of jeans selling individually for £30 for £50, or one pair of the jeans and a £20 t-shirt for £40. It presents the illusive feeling of value for the shopper and if you've ensured you're still making your desired profit, can be a very effective pricing model. Buy one get one free food menus are another prime example, where the profit made on the cost of drinks for two people almost always generates enough to compensate for any profit sacrificed to entice people through the door.

Round down pricing

There's also a school of thought that shoppers round down a price instead of rounding it up, so it's better to price goods at £9.99 not £10. That's increasingly dismissed now though and some shops actually play on the notion of transparency and honesty of a rounded £10 price tag. In reality, other than all those missing pennies, it's unlikely to make a massive difference. If you're able to drop prices to, say, £9.49, than perhaps the argument becomes relevant again.

Discount pricing, sales and price reductions

These are also a crucial part of pricing strategy and certainly shouldn't be confined to traditional sales' periods such as January. Neither should it be viewed as a way of shifting dead stock.

Loss leaders

The most effective and common discount pricing method in retail, and the one that causes the biggest challenge for small shops competing with large changes and supermarkets, are loss leaders.

The idea is that by pricing one in demand item at cost price (or even below), you'll entice customers who will buy more than just that item. You'll have noticed supermarkets frequently competing for the lowest price for staple goods.

Cost-plus pricing or mark-up pricing

These are the terms commonly given to deciding your own profit amount or percentage to be added to its cost; it is likely to be where you'll start but it shouldn't be your only consideration. Most successful pricing strategies will include several of the pricing policies and almost always at the same time. This can be confusing, but always revert to the basic principle of knowing what you're paying and what you're making at the price you're selling at. Stick to that and you can't go wrong.

➡ CALCULATING EXPENSES AND BUDGETING

When you're working out your costs you need to plan for the first 12 months. That landmark first anniversary might seem a long way off when you're sitting there with an idea and a pile of research, but it's essential to consider not just your start-up costs but ongoing overheads for the first year. Many companies break these down into one month, six month and then first year budgets.

For a full budget and to see how viable your business is you'll need to balance revenue forecasts against costs. We'll come to forecasting later but it's just as crucial to work out and keep track of how much you're spending, not just the sales you hope to get through the till. Without expenses any forecasts or even sales prove very little as far as how profitable your shop can be.

IN MY EXPERIENCE:

Clare Thommen, Boudiche

Our sales weren't as much as we'd forecast for the first few months and cashflow was a real struggle as a result. We had no cash buffer and I wish someone had helped us be more realistic at the start.

The good news is that it's far easier to work out reliable costings than revenues, especially if you veer on the side of caution.

Begin by looking at all your initial start-up costs. All the costs of getting your shop up and running go into the start-up expenses category. These expenses may include:

- business registration fees
- initial stock
- rent deposits
- down payments on property
- down payments on equipment
- shop fitting costs
- utility set up fees

This is just a sample list and you probably won't have trouble adding to it once you start listing your costs.

Your operating costs are those expenses that your business will incur on an ongoing basis; essentially what you'll need to pay out each month. They may include:

- your salary
- staff salaries
- rent or mortgage payments
- telecommunications
- utlities
- stock

- storage
- distribution
- promotion
- loan payments
- office supplies
- maintenance
- professional services (ie accountancy fees)

Again, this isn't a complete list and outgoings will vary from month to month. However, once you've completed your own lists you should have a fairly good idea, even if they're ballpark figures, of what revenues and/or funding you're going to need to support your business over a month, six month and yearly basis.

These figures should go into a financial budget plan towards the end of your business plan which also takes into account, of course, how much money you can realistically make.

➡ MAKING REVENUE FORECASTS

Sales forecasting is notoriously difficult and the point where many business plans fall down. Almost always that's because either the business owner is hopelessly optimistic or the plan only succeeds in proving the business isn't viable because of the number of sales needed to generate a profit, the cost goods would need to be priced at is unrealistic or the cost of sustaining the business until it breaks even is unsustainable.

The biggest challenge is that you don't have any previous sales history to guide you. This is hopefully where your market research can help with examples of average sales volume per square foot for similar shops in similar locations and of a similar size. Also consider how many people there are within certain distances and what percentage of their disposable income you can reasonably hope to secure.

However, this isn't entirely adequate as it's highly unlikely you'll perform at a similar level for perhaps up to a year.

The simplest forecast is to start by working out what you hope to be selling within six months. Work this out per unit per day so you have a gross sales figure and multiply that by the number of opening days in a month. Next look to scale proportionately from month one, where you're unlikely to have many sales, upwards to month six. You can then extrapolate that scale over 12 months for an annual sales forecast.

In addition to that one forecast, carry out the process three times with a pessimistic, optimistic, and realistic outlook. Next try and put a real-time calendar next to your 'month one', 'month two' etc taking into account the peaks and troughs in trade you anticipate and is suggested from your research. Many shops see huge variations season-by-season, if not month-by-month, with many taking over half their annual profits during the build-up to Christmas, at the peak of the summer holiday season or in the January sales.

> **FROM THE EXPERTS:**
> ## Mike Clare, Dreams plc
>
> I used to do one set of figures for the banks, one for the board and one for staff targets but you're never quite sure which one you're benchmarking against so it's better to just be fair and honest with yourself and about you think you're realistically going to do.

Compiling a financial sheet

Once you've worked out your financial outgoings (both initial start-up and ongoing costs) you can put the two together to produce a clearer analysis of the viablitiy of your shop on paper and when your business will break even.

Begin by compiling month-by-month expenses and sales forecasts. In the same way you accounted for peaks and troughs in sales, look at months where you expect expenses to be higher than others. For instance, if you cater for the Christmas rush you may buy far more stock in September, October and November than other months of the year and try to look ahead to large one-off purchases for equipment or perhaps a vehicle.

Again, ensure you prepare three income/outgoings projections: pessimistic, optimistic, realistic. Also try and account for the fact that the price you can purchase stock for will hopefully decrease as your sales levels increase. However, that's a calculation you probably want to reserve for your optimistic forecast unless you've already got such an agreement in place from suppliers.

> ### IN MY EXPERIENCE:
> ## Paul Mather, Sherston Post Office Stores
>
> We did four forecasts. One based on previous trends, one slightly ambitious, one very ambitious and a 'doomsday scenario' which involved Tesco opening on our doorstep and slashing costs and staff to a minimum.

While your calculation will inevitably alter from month-to-month (something you'll need to be wary of when managing cashflow) the point where your sales equal your expenses is where you 'break even' and hopefully go on to generate profit.

There are some accepting formulas used to demonstrate this:

Break-Even Point (£) = Fixed Costs ÷ Gross Margin Percentage

For example: A retail store buys portable fans for £10 each, marks them up and sells them for £20. Their monthly expenses (fixed costs) are £12,000. This means our breakeven point would be £24,000 or 667 units.

£12,000 ÷ (10/20) = £24,000

This level of information should give you a much more powerful overview of not just how viable your business is, but what funding is required and when. It also enables you to pre-empt when you may need assistance with cashflow or credit.

Having this at your fingertips won't just impress investors and the banks but should also give you a much firmer grasp on your buying decisions when it comes to actually finding and fitting out premises. But first of all, go back to the start of this section and make sure it's all safely listed in your business plan!

Plan financially month-by-month but be wary of how much stock you carry. It's a common retail tendency to overstock and give too much choice to the customer. Take a cooler overview, keep money in reserve and commit no more than 50% of sales forward.

Things to remember:

- Don't just write your business plan for your investors, use it as your main guide for the direction of the business.

- Include all the necessary detail but don't overload it. A good plan is thorough but succinct.

- Be realistic with your sales forecasts. It's better to underestimate than overestimate.

- Have three different trading forecasts – pessimistic, optimistic and realistic.

S culpting the identity of your business should be one of the most enjoyable challenges when starting your shop and is probably something you've already given a great amount of thought to. You need to do more than think about it though. It has to form a major chunk of your start-up planning.

Planning the identity of your shop means planning everything which will make up the experience of your customers, from the physical layout of the premises to the type of food you will serve. The other major detail you have to make a decision about is what to call your shop. Think about your aspirations – if you want to expand and build a brand, best not call your shop by the place name. Remember, lots of people try and be TOO clever. It's most important to convey what your shop sells, and to appeal to your customer base.

In this chapter we'll look at:

- Choosing a name
- Logos and themes
- Establishing your identity
- What your brand stands for

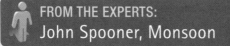 CHOOSING A NAME

For one of the least technical aspects of starting a business, picking a name for your shop could prove frustratingly tricky. For some of you, owning a shop with your name above the door was part of the dream from day one or the name could have been core to the vision; but for others you'll agonise over it, then kick yourself relentlessly for wasting time over something that will eventually seem so obvious.

Business names are funny things and their importance polarises opinion. It's easy to understand the ambiguity. Think of any successful retailer, brand or product that you buy from and in almost every instance, the name is the very last consideration and least important factor in your conscious buying decision.

> **FROM THE EXPERTS:**
> ## John Spooner, Monsoon
>
> Get some paper, wine and a thesaurus and sit down with friends. Then check out it's not being used by anyone else and return to the red wine if it has. Avoid anything insensitive or too controversial if that clashes with your identity, but remember it's the product and experience that is most important.

That said, business names are how we all identify and refer to those shops and products and it's often what we remember most. And while some names bear little significance to anything, the smartest names undoubtedly form part of the branding and identity that pulls us in.

How important are business names?

It's safe to assume that you won't improve a poor shop with a great name, and a great shop shouldn't suffer too badly from an average moniker. Let's face it, what you sell, for what price and how good your service is will determine whether people like your shop or not.

But that doesn't mean names aren't important.

A good name will:

- Draw attention and attract people through the door
- Communicate a clear message about your shop's identity
- Lend itself well to PR and set you aside from the competition

A poor one will hinder all of the above. So they're the basic four principles you should work on when planning a name.

Regional and web friendly names

Regional names can work if you don't have aspirations of expanding or relocating. Locals might consider they're supporting a town's trade if you carry its name. If you're selling products in an area which is renowned for it, it also makes sense to take advantage of that reputation. For instance, if you're selling fudge or clotted cream in Cornwall using the name of the county or even a town, let's say 'St Ives Fudges & Creams', lends you greater credibility with tourists than say 'Smith's Fudges & Creams' or 'Delicious Fudges & Creams'. That's unless your great uncle Smith invented fudge, of course!

You'll also need to think about web presence when considering the suitability of a name. Even if you're not thinking of selling online, it's so easy and cheap to get a website to publicise your business that you'd be foolish not to at least consider it as a future option. Regional names will allow locals to find your website when they search with location included. However, it can also work against you. If you're called 'Nottingham Silks Ltd', you're sure to appear for a 'Nottingham + Silks' search but will you get lost amongst all the other results? Here a unique name could work to ensure you appear, get seen and people can also find you when they type in your name.

> ### TIP
> When thinking about names that'll work on the internet, think search. Nine tenths of visitors to all websites arrive via a search engine. For search, read Google. Some names will work well for shops, but will impact differently in search.

To the other extreme, don't make the mistake of naming your company simply because it's a well-searched word or term. It's not about appearing on the most searches, just the right ones and near enough to the top. Andrew Selby had to rebrand his iPod accessories company because the original name, I-magine, (a clever enough name as a shop), returned nothing but John Lennon search results.

Avoid obvious clangers as well. I once received a press release from a new business selling a product which safely adjusted adult seatbelts for children. Thinking it sounded like a decent enough product with market potential I read on only to discover the numbskull behind it had ruined a perfectly good business with the name 'Cruising4Kids'. And of course, I wasn't even going to risk looking at the website. In case you're equally scared to check, the url is still being used but by a cruise ship firm – just as terrible!

How to think of a name

With all this in mind, possibly the best bet is how most entrepreneurs say they came up with their business' name: brainstorming it around a table, preferably in a pub or, if at home, with a glass of wine. Set those creative juices flowing and see when what you can come up with.

The obvious place to start is semantics. Find a word that encompasses what your business either sells or represents. For instance, think about how Habitat represents what it sells or Virgin with the attitude it aimed to exude and audience it hoped to inspire. You don't have to come up with something clever though and the high street is littered with names that have vague or little relevancy to the items sold. You don't pop into Currys for a tikka masala for instance and last time I checked Carphone Warehouse isn't a warehouse and doesn't sell carphones.

Something that people will remember should be high on your criteria. Businesses have used evocative words, words you wouldn't expect to see used alone, acronyms, people's names, colours in a bid to grab attention and memory. EAST, NEXT, ORANGE, Tossed, FCUK, all spring to mind as examples that work.

> **FROM THE EXPERTS:**
> ## Mike Clare, Dreams
>
> It's got to be a name you can pronounce and understand. We were going to be called Bucks Beds but we couldn't have opened in Wales with that. When we changed from Sofa Bed Centre to Dreams, my accountant was against it because it didn't say what it did, but that's why he's still an accountant and I'm an entrepreneur. I love it and knew it'd work for a chain.

Whatever you do, don't waste your money paying someone to come up with a name: there's no shortage of companies that will do this but it's simply not a wise way to spend money as a start-up. If you're still not convinced, take heed from Royal Mail's calamitous multi-million pound rebrand to Consignia. Okay we're only talking names here not full branding, but it's a fair bet if Royal Mail had taken a tenth of the money it paid for the rebrand and offered it to its staff to come up with a new identity, they'd have come up with something a lot better.

IN MY EXPERIENCE:
Lance Prebble, Pole Position

Our name is everything. It's intrinsically linked to the brand and the aspirations of our customers. The shop would be a far weaker proposition without it.

Chances are you'll change your mind before you open anyway so don't worry too much. For several months Cobra Beer was named Panther, until the company's market research suggested it wasn't liked. Cobra's more than proved its name works but its founder Lord Karan Bilimoria is unable to offer any explanation as to why it's preferable to Panther.

Bilimoria thinks naming is an intangible science and it quite possibly is. Certainly, bar a few obvious clangers, a name that encompasses what you do, is memorable, and most importantly feels right is what you're aiming for. Remember, it won't make or break your business, but choose it carefully because it's likely you'll have to live with it as rebrands are notoriously risky and expensive.

TIP

If you decide to incorporate your business you need to make sure you pick a name nobody else has. If you run your business as a sole trader this is not as much of an issue but you still need to be aware of the legal implications of choosing an offensive moniker, or one with certain banned words. Check Registering Your Business for more on the legal aspects of choosing a name.

⇒ WHAT IS YOUR IDENTITY?

Sculpting the identity of your business should be one of the most enjoyable challenges and is probably something you've already given a great amount of thought to. No doubt you had a vision when you first embarked on this journey of you standing behind the counter running your quaint little shop or ultra modern fashion boutique.

You shouldn't lose sight of that vision. It's quite possibly changed a little from the planning stage where you further identified USPs, pricing strategies and differentiators, but essentially it's still that vision, combined with these factors, that makes up your shop's identity.

It's certainly not just the products you sell (or the prices you charge) that will determine whether you get people through the door and money through the till. You'll need to create a location and environment that pulls customers and encourages them to spend.

IN MY EXPERIENCE:

Clare Thommen, Boudiche

The identity was a core part of the initial idea for us. It's about luxury and extravagance and that has to come across in bedroom boudoir feel of the boutiques, the website and branding.

Too many shop owners don't communicate that identity, however. For some reason they have it in their head but lose sight of it when actually building the shop. That's where the discipline of being a business person as well comes in.

Don't neglect your USPs

Keep going back to those USPs: other than the pure products it sells, what is your shop? What will it look and feel like. If it's upmarket premium goods you're selling to a customer with a high disposable income then the identity; from logo to location, price to packaging; should reflect that. In turn, if you sell eco goods or ethically sourced products you'll want that to be entwined in all that you do.

Many businesses talk about core values and many entrepreneurs like to draw up a list of values that reflect their shop's identity as a reminder to themselves and staff. It can certainly pay to constantly revisit them to ask: is this what we're about? Are we sticking to our USPs?

Once you sacrifice those USPs – start selling different products simply because you think you can make a nice return; compromise on quality to generate sales etc – your shop stops becoming what you started it to be.

This can be particularly difficult during the difficult early days of trading and fitting out, but your whole sales story has been built on a unique identity and losing sight of it is a major, but commonly made, mistake.

Artistic theme and logos

You should scope out the identity of your business before you commit time or funds to a logo or an artistic theme as they should communicate identity, and your USPs, to your customers at all times.

Your logo is one way people will remember you and it's certainly how many customers will form their first impression of you. Images and colours are very powerful methods of communicating messages and you want to think carefully about the logo that should emblazon your shopfront, signage, plastic/paper bags, packaging receipts, advertising, PR, company brochures, potentially uniforms.

That said, please don't rush out and commission are brand identity group. It's often just a case of finding a logo which simply and clearly radiates your business identity. The fuller brief you can write about what your shop is, who your customers are and what your USPs are, the closer a designer will be able to produce something close to what you're looking for. It's a subjective decision of course though, so it's always an idea to give an example of logos you like and don't like.

If you're looking to launch straight onto the high street directly up against the big name competition and have a bit of money to play with, it could be worth seeking a professional consultant who can carry out some market research around designs that work in this space and with focus groups. It won't be cheap, but you'll be getting professional advice.

> **FROM THE EXPERTS:**
> ## John Spooner, Monsoon
>
> If you've the resources then it's nice to get something well packaged from day one, but remember the customer buys the product and experience first. Monsoon has probably changed their logo six times.

Alternatively a logo created by a freelance designer or small design company might give you the independent edginess that makes you stand out. For most of you you'll have no option but to pursue this route. Another is ask local design colleges or students to submit entries, incentivising them with a prize or vouchers for the shop once it's open. There are a number of websites for budding, freelance or small design companies where you can pitch such competitions or request enquiries, with www.logosauce.com probably being the best. Just post your brief (remember to be as detailed as possible), set a deadline then wait for 'bidders' to upload their best efforts and contact the ones you like.

> ## TIP
>
> Having a number of designs to choose from certainly helps you decide what works well, so even if you decide to give the project to one person or company ask them to give you at least a couple of options and colour schemes. You're likely to favour one and then ask to see several variations of that until you're happy.

Logos should work well in a number of sizes; whether it applies to you or not, think postage stamp and billboard. They should work well online as well as offline even if you're still in denial about the need for a website; and forward plan to ensure what works for you as a start-up will work for you are burgeoning retail chain. Even if this isn't your goal, it'll almost certainly be how many of your customers will want to see you.

One note of caution about artistic themes: don't make the mistake of thinking everyone shares your idea of good taste and smart design. They won't. This isn't your house you're choosing a theme for, it's your shop. While it might be 'yours' its success will be dependent on others wanting to go there, so unless you're selling the type of product that lends itself to the weird and wonderful, remember that niches are niches for a reason. Instead, apply the property development mantra: design for the broadest range of people you're looking to sell to as possible.

Do your research, get out and look at how your competition style their identity and visit larger shops to see what they get right. Also force yourself to study a successful retailer whose identity doesn't particularly appeal to you and consider what it is that makes it work for its shoppers.

As a rule though: create a detailed brief, get a number of designs to choose from and go with what works best for your customer, not you.

What does your brand stand for?

Branding differs from identity as it focuses more on what people think of your business and what it stands for. Whether you like it or not, people will form opinions about your shop from the minute it opens. They'll form opinions on what it looks like, the products it sells, the attitude and turn-out of you and your staff and assign it, consciously or not, among the other brands they're exposed to and buy from.

How much you care about branding is likely to be dependent on how much you intend to grow your business. If your sole ambition is open a shop and make a nice living from it, you probably don't need to think too much about building a brand, simply maintaining your reputation in your local community should suffice. If your intentions are to one day establish a chain of shops then branding needs to be at the fore of your thinking.

> **FROM THE EXPERTS:**
> ## Mike Clare, Dreams Plc
>
> It's a case of revisiting those USPs. Our three mantras are largest selection, lowest prices, fastest delivery and everything we do should build on that.

Either way, return sales will be crucial so you should be thinking about how people think about your business, and that means more than just the physical shop. It's the way you treat customers, the level of interaction you look to have post-sale and how you communicate in your advertising or marketing.

Some brands are heritage brands, such as Harrods, that feed off the grandiose of years of trading the richest and finest products and traditional British retail excellence. The fact it's now owned by an Egyptian who's dragged the Royal Family through the court system has done little to diminish its reputation as an internationally renowned shopping location.

In turn, exciting new innovative companies and shops shape themselves firmly as cutting edge brands taking on the old establishment with a better, fresh approach.

Deciding what your brand should stand for is about considering how you want people to view you. That should come, essentially, from who your customer is and what you're looking to sell. If you've researched your customer fully you should have a clear idea of their tastes, the ways they prefer to shop, the experiences they like and in turn don't like and that should give you a clear idea of how you should look to position your brand to them and the outside world.

Branding for you as a start-up shop owner shouldn't be a massive pre-occupation but as it's closely aligned to what your identity and overall sales story is it is a very worthwhile exercise trying to draw up a list of words you'd like others to describe you with. This will make a useful reference document to refer back to when making buying decisions and help form marketing decisions and, eventually, a fuller branding strategy.

Things to remember:

- Remember that identity must go hand-in-hand with every aspect of your planning.

- Don't agonise over your shop's name but do give it careful consideration.

- Spend some time on your logo, but not necessarily lots of money.

- Keep your branding as consistent as possible.

O pening up a shop is a costly business, but is very doable with the right planning and financial backing.

The internet has allowed a whole generation of entrepreneurs to make their millions with virtually no start-up capital. Online retailers are having a field day. However, your dream of opening a physical shop is not one where you can start trading without significant financial investment in the venture, so you're going to need to consider your funding opportunities carefully.

Although the prospect of making a presentation to a bank to convince them to fund your venture can seem daunting, this chapter outlines everything you need to do to prepare, from reviewing your business plan to what you should wear and how to cope if you hear that dreaded 'no'. Also covered are other means of finance which you should consider such as loans from friends and family or private equity finance, and how to protect yourself and your business if you choose this option.

In this chapter we'll cover:

- Finance options
- Friends and family loans
- Equity finance
- Banks
- Applying for a loan
- Pitching for finance
- Paying yourself

➡ FINE OPTIONS

retail on the internet and the number of new internet-only
The proc become retail giants in their own right, together with a decline
brandst shops in many sectors should tell you everything about the cost
of inf'shop.
of stmoney. Quite a bit of it. If you're looking to start a retail business
barriers to entry, have a couple of thousand to spend and don't want to
w anything, then you probably should be looking at an online model.
ne you can target a global audience (not that it meals they'll find you, but
nyway . . .) for very little outlay and you'll have none of the ongoing costs
you've identified in your business plan.

That said, shops still have plenty of upsides and, as we've already identified,
every chance of prospering. There's no getting away from it though, it's going to
cost you a pretty penny to get up and running and will also involve substantial
overheads. Certainly, for the vast majority of you it won't be a casual outlay as
many web operations start off as.

It's likely you'll have three funding options for opening a shop. The first is to
fund it yourself, the second to use a bank, the third to seek equity investment
from private investors. It's highly unlikely you'll raise venture capital finance to
start your first shop; possibly to roll-out a chain but not to start the first.

Funding it yourself

Funding it yourself should be a fairly simple decision: either you can or you can't.
There really is no such thing as free money so for pure efficiency nothing makes
better financial sense than resisting borrowing altogether. Of course it's an option
few are blessed with.

> **FROM THE EXPERTS:**
> ## John Spooner, Monsoon
>
> If you can do it by yourself, always, always take up this option. You should try and
> resist taking a loan out straight away and banks wouldn't be my first port of call,
> but that said, giving away equity should be your very last option.

It's also an option some are distinctly uncomfortable with. Do you really want to invest your life savings into a venture when it's possible to borrow from a bank? Possibly not. If that's the case, the first question to ask is if you're not convinced why should any other form of investor be? The second is how much can you comfortably put in? Banks are likely to expect you to match whatever they lend you and you'll do well to find an individual who'll give you their cash to play with while you keep your own in the bank.

> ### ✈ TIP
> ⚲ It can actually be sensible to fund start-up costs with a loan and save a slice of your own cash for running costs and future investment; borrowing for a loan will be less expensive than an overdraft or credit cards. There could also be tax advantages to structuring how much you invest yourself and borrow. This is the point where you should get an accountant on board who'll advise you on the best way to proceed.

Friends and family

'Fools' is often jokingly tagged onto the end of this duo and not just for its alliterative appeal. Start-up businesses are risky investments when they're backed by even the canniest of high yielding, wealthy business veterans. Yet strangely, people seem willing to part with princely sums for decisions based on little more than emotion, love and the conviction someone they believe in will look after their money.

As you're the one looking for the money, not blindly pumping it in, this might not concern you. Indeed, it's easy to turn the situation on its ear and let your determination to get your dream shop up and running convince you that you're actually doing them a favour by letting them share in your success. If all goes well, this could be true. It's what happens if it doesn't that you need to consider. Many friendships and relationships have gone out of the window as the bailiffs have walking in through the door, so think hard about selling too hard to friends and family. Explain the risks, get any investment tied up in a legally binding contract securing both your rights and express no matter how much you try to make this work you can't guarantee them it will.

If, after doing all this, both sides are happy then by all means go ahead. Funding from friends and family, when it works, is certainly a massive leg up and leaves you the freedom to save bank financing for a later stage when you're looking to expand and grow.

FROM THE EXPERTS:
John Spooner, Monsoon

If the opportunity is there, then why not give family and friends a chance to share in your success?

➡ EQUITY FINANCE

Before we look at banks, which are how most of you will fund the opening of your shop, it is worth touching on equity finance which is where you give away a percentage of your business in exchange for the money you require to start or grow.

Private equity usually comes from one or more private wealthy individuals commonly known as business angels who are often experienced entrepreneurs with money to invest in other up and coming companies. While the reality is far removed from the drama of the TV show, these are the kind of deals struck on BBC hit series Dragons' Den. It's also possible to raise equity finance through organised public or private funds which are usually run by either experienced entrepreneurs or investment companies. Private equity deals usually fill the gap between standard bank loans and venture capital deals, but can vary from anything from £10,000 to £250,000.

> ## ✦ TIP
>
> Equity finance is where you give away a percentage of your business in exchange for the money you require to start or grow.

Venture capital (VC) works on the same principal but is run by large organisations and deals are usually in excess of £500,000, although this is rare for start-up businesses, even rarer for new shops and the VC will usually place someone on the board.

Private equity is certainly more common but not easy to find and not always the advised route for initial start-up capital. A more recognised route is to start one shop using debt finance, perfect the business model and develop evidence of the business' potential to expand and then refinance using private equity. At that point, with solid evidence of sales, market and product supply, far more investors are likely to be interested.

However, if you've run a shop or business before or have a proven track record in retail management it might be that you'll find an investor willing to take a punt on you from day one.

> ## ✦ TIP
>
> There's one thing all our advisers agree on. If you can keep 100% to start with then do so. However, those in the investment world will no doubt argue it's way smarter to own 50% of a company worth £1m than 100% of one worth £100,000 – and clearly that's true.

The problem is that whatever you're giving away at the start won't be worth very much, so it's almost certain you'll lose a chunky slice at what in a few years time might seem a meagre sum. Far better to use debt finance and then refinance once you've a better position to bargain from and can offer a greater chance of reward for the investor's risk.

FROM THE EXPERTS:
Mike Clare, Dreams plc

Never ever let equity go. Definitely not. If you work with someone else there's a good chance you'll fall out. I very much believe in doing it yourself.

Taking on an equity partner also provides a new sense of responsibility and pressure. With the money comes a need to create a substantial return in an agreed period of time and once you commit to that the decisions you make must become more focussed on generating that return than what works for you in a lifestyle scenario. That can be a very healthy motivation and it's worth it if that's the type of business you want to run.

Regional venture capital funds

The Capital Fund: www.thecapitalfund.co.uk

South East Growth Fund: www.segrowthfund.co.uk

East of England Fund: www.createpartners.com

South West Regional Venture Capital Fund: www.southwestventuresfund.co.uk

Advantage Growth Fund: www.midven.com

East Midlands Regional Venture Capital Fund: www.catapult-vm.co.uk

Yorkshire and Humber Fund: www.yfmventurefinance.co.uk

Capital North East: www.nel-capital.co.uk

North West Fund: www.nwef.co.uk

> ### Sources of business angel funding
>
> Advantage Business Angels: www.advantagebusinessangels.com
>
> Beer & Partners: www.beerandpartners.com
>
> British Business Angel Association: www.bbaa.org.uk
>
> Envestors: www.envestors.co.uk
>
> Equus Capital: www.equuscapital.co.uk
>
> Great Eastern Investment Forum: www.geif.co.uk
>
> Hotbed: www.hotbed.uk.com
>
> London Business Angels: www.lbangels.co.uk
>
> North West Business Angels: www.nwbusinessangels.co.uk
>
> Pi Capital: www.picapital.co.uk
>
> SWAIN: www.swain.org.uk
>
> Yorkshire Association of Business Angels: www.yaba.org.uk
>
> Xenos: www.xenos.co.uk
>
> (NB: some sources only cover certain areas of the UK.)

➡ BANK OR DEBT FINANCE

Banks lent £33.3bn to small businesses in 2006 and contrary to the doom and gloom surrounding the state of the economy are still very much lending to people like you starting independent shops.

As such, they should be the first place you look when looking to finance your shop. Banks are vastly experienced in helping start-up shops and should be able to offer a number of finance packages tailored to suit your needs as well as a providing fair degree of support. A good bank manager should be able to give you a clear explanation of your options and what is expected to meet any lending criteria.

Be warned though, banks know shops and retail models inside out so will see through any overly optimistic forecasts, dressing up of figures or holes in your business plan so you'll need to ensure your research is comprehensive.

Choosing a bank

It's natural that you'll probably turn to your current bank first – and you shouldn't apologise for that. At least half of a successful banking relationship is the relationship not the bank. Indeed, it's often the relationship with the bank manager.

Different banks offer different incentives such as so many years' free banking to open a business bank account as well as pricing and organising their charging mechanisms differently. Some offer a greater level of service and usually offer lower interest rates or higher charges as a result, while other banks specialise in keeping basic costs low but offering little service.

Even if you're keen to stay with your main bank, do shop around and examine the start-up packages on offer, if only to check you're not missing out on something offered elsewhere. If you are, negotiate.

While there are savings it's likely you'll ultimately derive more long term value from finding a bank you're comfortable with; who makes the effort to listen and understand your business and, ultimately, will lend you the money you need to start-up.

Even if you've decided on a bank offering make sure you meet the bank manager you'll be dealing with. The relationship with your bank manager is absolutely fundamental to your success, especially in raising finance. Managers will have a threshold of loans they can sign off and even though you'll be assessed by the bank's credit and decisions programmes, having your manage onside will make a massive difference.

> ## ✦ TIP
>
> Be warned: bank managers will vary within banks not just from bank to bank. If you like a package at one bank but don't click with the manager, ask to see another. Alternatively, check your manager is experienced in retail and within your focus area; it could make a difference.

Accounts

Let's be clear, you need to know your numbers. At any point you should know how much money you've got in the pot, how much you owe, how much is in the till, what you're committed to in orders, salaries and rent, how much your assets (equipment, stock, property, vehicles) are worth and, if anything, how much you're owed. You should know what you've taken that day (preferably that hour) and what you're going to make for the rest of the hour, day, week, month, year.

You should know it and you should understand it. Otherwise you'll have no idea how the business is performing and no solid financial base from which to make decisions.

The basics you should understand are how to read a balance sheet of your income and outgoings, called a profit & loss sheet. Here's an example.

You certainly don't *need* to know much else, though. Sure it'll help, but not everyone is great with figures and that's what accountants are for. If you pay for any outside help in setting up your shop, an accountant with experience in the sector will almost certainly prove the most useful and offer the best return on investment.

If you think you'll need the services of an accountant do it early in the process. Too many take the option of chucking all their receipts in a shoebox and handing it over to the accountant when it comes to the end of the tax year and time to fill in your annual return. Sure, an accountant will sort his out for you but involve them early on and they'll get your financial data straight from the start and almost certainly find ways of making you some fairly significant savings.

Profit & loss example

For month ended 30/06/2008

	£	£
Sales/turnover		60,894
Opening stock (1st of Month)	3,000	
Add purchases	24,253	
	27,253	
Less closing stock (30/31st of month)	4,278	
Cost of goods sold	31,531	
Direct labour costs	7,364	
		38,895
Gross Profit		**29,363**
Overheads		
Rent and rates	3,294	
Heat, light and power	783	
Insurance	106	
Indirect wages and salaries	7,296	
Marketing costs	571	
Printing, stationery and consumables	951	
Computer costs	1,058	
Telephone	739	
Depreciation of assets	3,697	
Legal and professional fees	750	
Bank and finance charges	264	
		19,509
Net Profit Before Tax		**9,854**

Applying for a bank loan

Bank loans remain the most common and preferred type of finance for opening shops. The nature of acquiring and fitting out premises and purchasing stock on top of all the operational costs associated with starting any business, make shops cash-intensive to start up and quite often too much of an undertaking for someone to make on their own.

The upside is that the banks are familiar with financing loans for shops. They know retail models inside out and you won't have to try and convince them of a whole new concept or sector.

The downside to this is that banks also have very clear expectations of what they want to see from your business plan before they'll give you a penny and it's crucial you bear this in mind.

They'll want to see you've factored for all eventualities, your own income and been realistic about your anticipated revenues. Some entrepreneurs will tell you it's sometimes best to have two sets of figures: a real one for yourself and a dressed up one for the bank. That might work for industries such as the internet and web 2.0 where business models are still new and revenues emerging all the time, but banks know shops so any gilding of the lily is unlikely to wash.

> **FROM THE EXPERTS:**
> ## John Spooner, Monsoon
>
> You should carry out a degree of sensitivity analysis. I prefer to be very conservative when budgeting but admittedly this isn't always the best way to convince lenders. However, be too optimistic and you won't reach the targets you've set an expectation for.

That said, the banks will have a clear criteria you'll be expected to meet for them to convinced they'll see a return on their investment. If you're at all unsure about your forecasts or figures it's worth speaking to a bank manager before submitting any loan application to see if you're heading along the right line or need to have a rethink.

Depending on how much you want to borrow, banks will usually expect to see that you're matching what you're borrowing with your own money and could also ask for security against your home. This is something that puts many people

off and can seem understandably
frightening. If you reach this point and
are having second thoughts, you're
possibly not ready to start a business
after all. What you're about to do is
indeed high risk. However, providing

> **TIP**
>
> As a rule of thumb, banks are
> likely to expect to see security for all
> loans above £25,000.

it works it's also full of rewards. If you're not convinced that balance is in your
favour you have to ask why the bank should.

If you can't offer the security the bank is asking for, you could apply for a loan through
the government's Small Firms Loans Guarantee Scheme which guarantees bank loans
up to £250,000 and while notoriously bureaucratic and inconsistent in its outcome, is
welcomed by all the main banks and did support £? worth of loans last year.

If you're reluctant or unable to offer security or match the bank's lending the other
option is to lower the amount you want to borrow. Providing you've a decent credit
rating and can offer reasonable evidence you'll be able to afford the repayments,
banks will often give immediately sanctions to personal loans up to around £15,000
which can be used for start-up costs and repaid over 36–84 months.

Banks will also offer you credit card and overdraft facilities, but will discourage
you from using them for anything other than cashflow management and short
term borrowing. That's not to say you can't use them however you see fit but,
especially in the current climate, be very careful about borrowing anything you
couldn't afford to pay back at very short notice or you could find yourself in real
trouble over a relatively small amount.

➡ PITCHING FOR FINANCE

Before we get into the detail of what you should say, how you should dress and
what banks and investors expect when you pitch for finance, it's important to
highlight one all important, and too often overlooked fact about borrowing
money: banks (and investors) want to lend it.

That's right, regardless of how bad the economic climate gets, banks and
investors will always lend money if they're confident they'll get a healthy return.
Your challenge then isn't to beg and grovel for any scrap of money you can get
your hands on, but to present a compelling opportunity for them.

It's on this premise you should base your pitch. Remember banks are investing
other people's money so they need to, as closely as possible, guarantee a return.
They're certainly not gamblers. Your challenge then is to present a clear, low risk

proposition that demonstrates how the money will be spent and, crucially, how it'll be repaid and when. While investors might be entailing a slightly higher degree of risk and possibly expect to, they won't entertain anything but a sensible punt.

Preparation

Make sure you're 100% prepared. If you're actually making a presentation, be clear about all your facts and figures and know them off by heart. It's likely that a bank will have already read your business plan by the time you get to pitch or talk through your proposition.

View this stage as good news that the bank wants to talk further. However, think what else they might want to ask you. Critique your own business plan or ask others to do it for you with a view to pre-empting any questions that stand out.

A clear concise answer will reassure the bank you're clear about what you're doing and that this matters to you sufficiently to have put the effort in. Don't attempt to try and answer a question if you can't; this only sends a message that you'll try and fudge. All investors prefer honesty so be honest and admit you don't know, but suggest you could certainly find out. Perhaps even flatter them by thanking them for bringing it your attention.

Appearance

Dress smart. If you don't wear a suit put on a smart shirt and trousers. That how you dress not how talented you are or how great your business idea is might determine if you get a bank loan or not is a contentious issue for many people. For others, wearing a suit demonstrates a professionalism and desire to be taken seriously. Whatever your personal view, from my experience the majority of bank managers will still expect you to dress smart so neglecting to do so is risky. If you're someone who simply couldn't bear to change their appearance then by all means dress as you see fit, but be aware one of the most important attributes of a small business owner needs to be flexibility and your reluctance to adapt could be viewed as representative of your personality.

Otherwise, if you go into the room feeling confident you've put your homework in, have belief in your idea and are looking smart there's every chance the bank will believe you're the type of individual they're looking for. And every chance they won't . . .

Dealing with a 'No'

Rejection is something you should get used to quickly. There's every chance several banks will say 'no' before one says yes. See each rejection as a learning experience or rehearsal for the one that says yes.

Find out why they've said 'no', the feedback might be useful. Don't let it dampen your spirits though, there's always more money out there. And don't argue with the decision either. Disputing a bank's decision to say no is as futile as arguing with refereeing decisions; you're never going to change their minds.

➡ PAYING YOURSELF

Your business plan should include how and what you intend to pay yourself for at least the first year – and it's essential you include this in any borrowing that you take out.

It's true that banks and investors love to see you're making massive sacrifices to see your business get off the ground. If you can afford not to take a salary for the first few months, even year, they'll expect you to do this. It not only ensures all profits can be reinvested back into the business, but demonstrates just how badly you want to succeed.

> **FROM THE EXPERTS:**
> ## John Spooner, Monsoon
>
> Ideally you shouldn't be looking to take anything out of the business for the first six months to a year. If you have to it's far more tax efficient to take it in the form of a dividend than a salary, but of course, that's not always possible if you've family responsibilities. Just live on as little as you can.

That said, it's simply impossible for many people to do this and starting a shop isn't just for people wealthy enough to have six months' salary in the bag. If you can't survive without taking a salary out of the business, whatever you do, don't pretend you can. Trying not to pay yourself and hoping you'll somehow meddle through almost never works and is foolish to try.

Everybody has to pay a mortgage or rent; everybody has to eat; everybody has reasonabe living expenses – and lenders do understand that. Not paying yourself a wage will just mean you end up borrowing elsewhere and, conversely, lenders can actually view that as bad management. Saying you can live on £500 a month when your mortgage is £1,000 a month isn't going to look too clever.

Lenders also dislike it when they lend an initial amount of money based on forecasts they've been told are realistic only for the borrower to promptly return needing more. Again that doesn't speak much for management.

It's far better to include your wage as a cost of the business. Indeed, it actually sets your business out on a solid model from the outset. Anyone who stepped into your shoes or acquired the business would expect to either earn a wage or pay a managing director a wage and your business model needs to be able to support that. For example, a business that claims to be generating a healthy profit of £50,000 but whose owners are effectively working for free, perhaps isn't as successful as it might first appear.

That said, don't expect to pay yourself a fortune. Investors won't appreciate you pulling up at the bank asking for a loan in a Ferrari dressed head to toe in Armani. If you're coming from a corporate background to escape the pressured rate race, be realistic. You're moving into retail and should expect to earn a retail salary.

> ### TIP
> So what's realistic to pay yourself? There are very few statistics for average earnings, but look at the average earnings of advertised posts retail manager and try and come in somewhere just below.

Things to remember:

- Consider your finance options carefully. What's best for you, straight loans or giving away a share of the pie?

- Make sure family and friends are clear about what they're getting involved in before you accept any cash from them.

- Be prepared when pitching. You need to know your figures inside out.

- Be realistic. It's better to ask for the cash in advance than ask for help when you're in trouble.

2

Setting up

Things to consider when financing a new retail business

1. How much finance is required?

First, you need to identify the equipment you require and the equipment suppliers you wish to use. It's possible to finance all business equipment including: EPOS, shop fittings, CCTV, joinery, air conditioning, furniture, signage etc. for your business. The general rule is: 'If it's for business use, it can be financed'. Make sure you factor everything you need including building works/fabrication into your plan. Once you have a rough idea of total set up cost, you can look to secure finance. It's possible to approve finance within 24 hours. For a new start shop, it's possible to approve anything from £1,000 to £250,000.

2. What information is required?

In order to secure finance, you'll need to supply basic information about yourself and your business. This information includes: what you want to finance, the amount of finance you require, your home address, date of birth, proposed opening date etc. If you have any other information that will support your application, now is the time to provide it. Examples of supporting information include: business plan, financial projections and details of your personal investment in the shop. At this stage you'll also need to confirm whether you're looking for finance over 3, 4 or 5 years.

3. What happens next?

Once you've provided all the relevant information about the business, you'll need to wait for formal finance approval (typically 24 hours). Once approved, paperwork is posted out directly for you sign. Once you've signed and returned paperwork, payment can be made directly to your chosen suppliers via bank transfer. The whole process from initial phone call to release of cleared funds can be completed within 7 days. Your monthly payments are fixed (inflation resistant) and 100% tax deductible. Payments are processed monthly by direct debit from a nominated account.

To talk to Portman Asset Finance about your new business, call on **0844 800 88 25**. Alternatively visit **www.portmanassetfinance.co.uk**

Registering your business

N aturally your energies will be focused on getting your shop open and trading – but before you can start searching for premises and fitting them out, you'll need to register your business. What can seem an overly complicated and laborious process isn't actually that difficult once you've established the basics and gathered all the information you'll need to register.

You'll need to decide what legal structure your business will take, complete the necessary paperwork and then submit your registration to Companies House, one of its licensed agents or HMRC.

To make life easier, this chapter will take you through the process in easy-to-absorb bite-size chunks so that even if you're not remotely business-minded you'll soon be back focused on 'shop' not 'business'.

In this chapter we'll cover:

- Sole traders and partnerships
- Limited companies
- Registering as a limited company

➡ THE DIFFERENT LEGAL STRUCTURES

There are essentially three legal or accounting structures you can choose from when starting your shop. You can go it alone by being a sole trader, team up to form a partnership or operate a limited company. Choosing the right structure is important, so you'll need to give it some serious thought. It is possible to switch between different structures after you've started your shop. For example, you may start out as a sole trader, and then decide to register your business as a limited company or partnership. You will save yourself a lot of work if you establish the most appropriate business structure beforehand though. Below is an explanation of the different legal structures you can choose from when starting your shop and guidance on which structure is most suitable for both you and your shop.

Sole traders and partnerships

Registering as a sole trader, essentially just you on your own, is relatively straightforward, record-keeping is simple and you get to keep all the profits after tax. As a sole trader you are the single owner of your business and have complete control over the way it is run. However, and this is quite a crucial factor, the law makes no distinction between the business and you as the owner. This means you'll be solely responsible from your own personal wealth for any debts if the business runs into trouble. This differs to a limited company (which we'll come to) where debts, but also profits, are liable to the company not the individual.

If you choose to run your shop as a sole trader you must register as self-employed with HMRC within three months of your trading start date otherwise you could be fined and charged interest on any outstanding tax and National Insurance payments you owe.

If you're forming your business with one or more other people you need to register as a partnership. As with the sole trader model, each partner is responsible for any debts the business incurs. Each partner is also self-employed and receives a percentage of any returns from the business, which they are then taxed on. The partnership as well as the individuals within it must submit annual self-assessment returns to HMRC and keep stringent records on business income and expenses.

Starting a shop as a sole trader or partnership venture can prove the easier option initially, especially if you don't have ambitions for rapid growth. There is less paperwork involved and you will not need to register and send annual returns to Companies House. It is also much easier to withdraw funds from the business as, essentially, all profits make up your own earnings. However, as well as the financial liability that lies at your feet, as a sole trader it is much more difficult to grow the business and you may find it harder when dealing with creditors and suppliers.

Limited liability companies

Registering as a limited (Ltd) company is probably the best legal structure to go with if you have any intention of growing your shop beyond the smallest of operations. As well as offering you a degree of personal financial security should your shop run into financial difficulty, it will also give you more credibility when seeking finance or credit. Registering your shop as a limited company also makes tax and succession planning a lot easier.

If you expect your shop to maintain a healthy amount of trade and return high levels of profit you will definitely want to go with the Ltd model. Profits will be subject to corporation tax, which currently stands at half the 40% income tax rate you could end up paying as a high-earning sole trader. Limited companies pay corporation tax on profits and company directors are taxed as employees in the same way as any other people you employ.

A limited company is very different from a sole trader model where there is no legal distinction between you and the business. A limited company is a separate legal entity to the people that run it. Profits and losses belong to the company, and the business can continue regardless of the death, resignation or bankruptcy of the shareholders or directors. Your personal financial risk will be restricted to how much you have invested in the company and any personal guarantees you gave when raising finance for the business. However, if the company fails and you have not carried out your duties as a company director, you could be liable for debts as well as being disqualified from acting as a director in another company.

> **TIP**
> If you decide to register your shop as a limited company you will need to allow more time to deal with the paperwork as it is a much more administration-heavy process than running a business as a sole trader. It will also require more stringent record keeping and auditing throughout the entire life of the business.

You get help with this from an accountant, of course, and if you have aspirations of your shop employing staff and making healthy profits (who hasn't?) a limited company is almost certainly the structure for you.

IN MY EXPERIENCE:

Paul Mathers, Sherston Post Office Stores

Our accountant did it and wasn't expensive. There are far more pressing things to do when you can get it done for you for a small price.

➡ REGISTERING AS A LIMITED COMPANY

To register your shop as a limited company you must submit the appropriate paperwork to Companies House, the official UK government register of UK companies or one of its registered formation agents. What follows is a guide to the process, documents and requirements involved in turning your business into a legal entity.

> **TIP**
> Companies House: Download all the forms you need to fill in at www.companieshouse.gov.uk. You can fill these in online, or send them to Companies House via post (see website for address).

Although it is possible to register a limited company yourself, unless you have done it before you are probably going to need to engage the services of a solicitor, accountant, chartered secretary or a company formation agent.

Formation agents use their own software that works directly with the Companies House systems. If you want to register your company electronically (most are registered this way) you will need to have the specific Companies House electronic interface – hence the need for a formation agent. However, you can still deliver the physical documents directly to Companies House without the need of a formation agent or specific electronic interface.

That's the official explanation, but in my experience it's far easier to register use an official formations agent and that's what most people do. There are lots of these agents listed on the Companies House website and all use slight variations of the same software. My advice would be to look at several and pick one that sound the most helpful or whose online system looks the easiest to use, providing the prices are sensible.

IN MY EXPERIENCE:

Clare Thommen, Boudiche

We registered as a limited company with an agency who now acts as our company secretary. It was pretty straightforward, but it is important to learn your obligations as a company director – or you could face jail if you get it wrong!

Costs

Prices for formation agents can cost up to £200 depending on the level and speed of service you require. A key advantage of using a formation agent is the advice they can give you on the compiling of the necessary documents and the right structure for your business. Companies House does not provide this service when registering, so if you are unfamiliar with the process it is advisable to get help to avoid errors. Going through the registration process yourself can be time-consuming, especially if you make a mistake, and Companies House staff will not advise you about specific matters such as the content of the documents you are required to submit.

Alternatively, you could also get assistance from an online registration company. The standard service usually costs £30-£100 including fees, but since some documentation needs to be posted, registration usually takes three to eight days, although there a few same-day services now coming onto the market. This option is usually cheaper than using a formation agent, although you will not receive the same level of personal service.

Finally, you can buy an 'off the shelf' company. You will receive a ready-made limited company that has designated company officers listed on the paper work. You simply transfer your name, and the names of any other company directors once you receive your documentation. The process can be completed on the same day and many accountancy firms will have several ready-made limited companies which they can sell to you. This is the quickest option, and with the exception of registering the company yourself, can often be the cheapest too.

TIP

It's worth noting that it costs as little as £15 to register directly with Companies House so what you're paying for is the service of an agent to help you through the process or an online agent's software.

Company officers

Once you have established whether or not you need help in establishing your company you will need to decide on who the company officers will be, and what your business will be called.

Limited companies are required by law to have named company officers. Company officers are the formally named directors and company secretary as stated in the Articles of Association, one of the documents you submit to Companies House which is explained in more detail below. It is a legal requirement for company officers to be in place at all times and for their names and current addresses to be written on the registration documents. If there is a change in company officers, Companies House must be informed straight away. All private limited companies must have at least one director and a company secretary.

Company directors – these are the people that manage the company's affairs in accordance with its Articles of Association and the law. Generally, anyone can be appointed company director and the post does not require any formal qualifications. However, there are a few exceptions:

You are prohibited from being a company director if:

- You are an undischarged bankrupt or disqualified by a court from holding a directorship
- You are under 16 (this only applies in Scotland)

Company directors have a responsibility to make sure certain documents reach the registrar at Companies House. These are:

- Accounts
- Annual returns
- Notice of change of directors or secretaries
- Notice of change of registered office

Directors that fail to deliver these documents on time can be prosecuted and are subject to fines of up to £5,000 for each offence. On average, 1,000 directors are prosecuted each year for failing to deliver accounts and returns on time so it is not a responsibility that can be taken lightly or ignored.

Company secretary – this person's duty is not specified by law but usually contained within an employment contract. For private limited companies, secretaries are not required to have any special qualifications.

The main duties of a company secretary are to:

- Maintain the statutory registers
- Ensure statutory forms are filed promptly
- Provide members and auditors with notice of meetings
- Send the Registrar copies of resolutions and agreements
- Supply a copy of the accounts to every member of the company
- Keep or arranging minutes of meetings

Naming your business

As well as establishing your company officers, you will also need to pick a company name to register the business with. The name of your business does not have to be the same as the name of your shop, however. If you open three shops, all with different names, you can still run them as one limited company. You will need to establish your company name before you think about filling out your registration documents as there are certain rules to consider.

The name you choose for you company must:

- Feature the word 'limited' or 'ltd' at the end. For Welsh companies the equivalent 'cyfyngedig' or 'cyf' can be used, but documentation must also state in English that it is a limited company.

- Not be made up of certain sensitive words or expressions (listed by Companies House) without the consent of the Secretary of State or relevant government department.
- Not imply a connection with central or local government.
- Not be offensive.
- Not be the same or similar to one that appears in the Index of Names kept by Companies House.

You can search the index of business names already registered on the Companies House website free of charge. If your chosen name is too similar to another, an objection can be lodged within 12 months following the incorporation of your company and you could forced to change it. See more about the process of choosing a company name and the legal implications that go with it, in the Identity chapter of Before you start on page 65.

Documents to submit

When registering a limited company there are four documents which must be provided to Companies House. These are:

Memorandum of Association

This document sets out the following:

- The company's name
- Where the company's registered office is located – England, Wales or Scotland
- What the company will do – this can be as simple as: 'to conduct business as a general commercial company'

Articles of Association

Here is where you set out the rules for running your company. You must state how shares will be allocated and transferred, how the directors, the secretary and your meetings will be governed. And if you decide not to adopt the standard articles of the Companies Act in full (known as Table A) you have to submit your amended version when registering. Once your company is incorporated you can only make changes if the holders of 75% of the voting rights in your company agree, so it pays to get this right at the outset.

Form 10

This document gives details of the first director(s), company secretary and the address of the registered office. Company directors must also give their name, address, date of birth, occupation and details of other directorships held in the last five years.

Form 12

This document is the statutory declaration of compliance with all the legal requirements of the incorporation of a company. It must be signed by either one of the company directors or secretary named on Form 10, or the solicitor forming the company. The signing of the document must be witnessed by a solicitor, a commissioner for oaths, a justice of the peace or a notary public. Form 12 must not be signed and dated before any of the other documents are completed, signed and dated.

Once all that's been submitted your shop is a fully-fledged limited company, but don't forget: the legal structure you choose when you start trading isn't set in stone. You can alter your structure, or even float on the stock market should your business become successful enough. For now though, you can concentrate once again on that first day of trading!

Things to remember:

- Assess your business structure options carefully. It may be cheaper to stay as a sole trader but are this risks to your personal finances worth it?

- When registering as a limited company make sure you've gone over your documents meticulously before submitting them. If you make a mistake you'll have to submit them again.

- Search the list of submitted business names on the Companies House website before you get your heart set on one. It may not be available.

Finding property

L ocating and securing the premises for your shop can be both exciting and frustrating – in fact, it almost certainly will be both of these. When you're actually looking around premises the vision of running your own shop seems to jump off the paper of your business plan and becomes a reality. Unfortunately, the flipside of that reality is finding a shop that meets your requirements and is affordable. In many instances it's impossible. There's a very good chance, as a start-up business, you won't get the ideal premises you identified in your business plan– it's more a case of setting the best of the rest!

You must decide what you need from your premises – in terms of size and layout and also in terms of how the location of your shop will impact on your profits. Once you have decided what type of property and what kind of area suit your needs you'll need to decide whether leasing or buying is best for you. There are advantages to both but for many, finance will be the key factor. This chapter also covers the legal issues of securing your premises such as the commercial classification and what kind of professional advice you should seek before moving forward on any decision.

In this chapter we'll cover:

- How to identify your property needs
- Commercial classifications
- Leasing vs buying
- How much it will cost
- Professional advisors
- Contracts

➡ WHAT ARE YOUR PROPERTY NEEDS?

At this stage you should already have a clear idea of what you require from your shop premises. You will have decided on the type of clientele you want to attract and the kind of atmosphere you want to create. You'll have also explored the demographics of your target customer, know how and where they spend their money and have a good understanding of the area where you're planning to open up.

In addition to all of this, you'll need to consider exactly what you'll need from your premises. How much floor space will you need, for instance? And how much space and what special requirements will you need for stock and storage? This will largely depend on the type of shop you're opening, of course. Beds take up considerably more space than books, but then furniture takes much less than looking after than frozen food items.

It's likely you'll need a small office for bookkeeping, records and dealing with suppliers in private; and also an area for staff to take their breaks, get changed and keep their coats and bags etc.

Try and plan this out. You can always create the necessary number of rooms and install special requirements but first and foremost you'll need to ensure you've got enough space overall – and, just as important, you're not paying for more than you need.

You can replace staff, change suppliers and tweak your business model. Property, however, is likely to be where you have least flexibility and at the most cost, so you'll want to get it right.

FROM THE EXPERTS:
Mike Clare, Dreams plc

It's unlikely you'll be able to afford prime location so look off prime but where people can still see you and park if that's important to your customers. Don't be too hidden away and use the money you save to promote awareness of where you are.

➡ LOCATION

Yes, you've heard it a million times: location, location, location. It really is everything when it comes to retail units. No retail location suits every shop so it's about deciding the location that best suits your shop – then when you realise you can't afford it or it's not available, finding the next one that suits it next best!

Your choice is essentially one of the following: high street, a shopping centre or retail park, secondary location or a station/or airport.

The high street

Also known in the property business as 'primary' or 'Zone A' locations, prime high street retail units are where you're likely to get the highest footfall figures (number of people passing by) and, consequently, where demand and price is also at its highest. The proliferation of bars and restaurants over the past 10 years has further increased competition for retail units and you'll not only find it difficult to afford a top spot, but also to secure it. Landlords are fussier because they can afford to be and the large retail chains often have units signed up before they get to market as they're constantly monitoring movement with a view to securing anything that comes available. Such is the competition you should actually treat units you can secure with caution – there will probably be a reason why it hasn't been snapped up. Don't fall into the trap of taking a badly positioned unit in a prime location just because you can secure it. It could prove a worse location than a prime spot in your second choice.

Shopping centres and retail parks

While the fad of out-of-town shopping centres seems to have cooled somewhat and towns are very much back in favour, shopping centres are still doing a good trade and certainly have their advantages. It's also worth noting the reservation of many town centres incorporate indoor shopping centres as key features. Parking and transport links are usually excellent and you're pitching to a captive audience who is there for one purpose and one purpose only: to shop. That said, like primary and Zone A units, the best locations in shopping centres aren't cheap and there are also a few stinkers. Be wary of units tucked away in quieter areas of the centre that attract limited passersby and, as a result of their low rents, are usually the home of pound shops and short lease come-and-go traders.

Secondary and tucked away locations

The obvious advantage to opening your shop somewhere less prominent is it's almost always cheaper. More quiet secluded areas are also likely to attract a different type of customer to that of the high street or retail park sites, and people will often travel longer distances and seek out hidden shops catering for a niche. However, if your business is operating in a mainstream space and relies on passing trade you may find it hard to pull in the customers. You will have to do far more promotion to inform customers of your presence if you want to attract more than just the local residents. The upside apart from cheap rent? Customers are more likely to be able to park.

Stations and airports

Britain's train and bus stations have become increasingly retail focussed over the past few years with a number of prime stations now boasting shopping centres rivalling any others within the city. It's easy to see the appeal of retail units within stations where commuters have no choice but to pass your door twice a day. With people increasingly working longer hours and searching for convenience, being able to incorporate shopping into their commute also makes the experience mutually appealing.

Convenience almost always comes at a price of course and most retail units charge a premium on goods. WH Smith charges around 10% more for soft drinks at station locations than standard high street stores (check), for example. More than aware of this, developers and landlords will attempt to pass this premium onto your rent, however, so you mightn't be that much better off.

Another interesting option popping up in stations are small stalls or sales stands. Breakfast company Moma (www.momafoods.co.uk) sells its healthy cereals, porridges and smoothies from behind a two man stand in London's Waterloo and Victoria stations. This can be a great, cost-effective way to prove a product before taking on a full lease.

Airports are another option for catching a captive shopper, however, retail units are often dominated by big players and luxury brands looking to cash in on holiday makers' high spirits and inclination to treat themselves and so it can be difficult to secure a pitch. You'll also need a proposition that naturally lends itself to the holidaymaker shopper.

Other considerations

Unfortunately, simply picking a location type rather simplifies matters and there are other considerations to take into account. Once you have decided what kind of location you want for your shop you'll need to consider the following factors:

- **Parking** – how easy is it for your customers to visit? Will you be selling goods that are too large or cumbersome to carry? If you are, parking is a must. It's no accident that retail parks with large open car parks are dominated by furniture and DIY stores.
- **Competition** – what other shops are in the area? Are they attracting the same kind of clientele you are after? Positioning yourself alongside the competition can make it tough to win customers. However, being located within a cluster of similar or complementary shops can also be an advantage as shoppers will come to the area for certain types of items in the knowledge they've a number of destinations to choose from.
- **Proximity to suppliers and delivery space** – you need to position your shop within easy reach of suppliers or where they have room to get to you. Getting hold of the right stock is crucial and if your shop is out of the way, suppliers may be reluctant to deliver, especially at short notice.
- **Proximity to staff** – if you want to attract the right level of talent for your shop you will need to make sure the location is both accessible and attractive for your staff.
- **Personal preference** – Lastly when choosing your location, think about whether you like it. You will be spending an awful lot of time in it. You need to be in an area that is accessible and agreeable to you too. Consider the unexpected. You might be used to commuting morning and evening, but suddenly it'll become your responsibility to be at the premises if the burglar alarms goes off at 3am and if it's genuine, you'll probably want to be there reasonably quick.

Lance Prebble, Pole Position

Regent Street is prime location and footfall is ridiculous but we still have to work to get people in the shop. Footfall also doesn't always equal shoppers. We're in a prime tourist area and this end of the street has more coffee shops and restaurants than prime retail so it's about psychology as well just numbers.

How long do you give it?

It's all very well deciding what premises you'd ideally like, but the reality is as a start-up you'll be resorting to second best anyway because the first choice is simply out of your price range. But what if you can't find somewhere among your second, or even third choices? Should you settle for somewhere that's not really what you identified above?

It's a tough call and one that could end up going either way. In some cases it makes sense to just get open. You can look at adapting or tailoring your marketing to compensate for a non-perfect location and if you do everything else right, people will keep coming back and spread the word. Occasionally shops actually benefit from being in a quirky location that makes them stand out in people's memory and pick-up extra customers that otherwise wouldn't pass them.

It's a risky strategy though and often it can simply pay to be patient even if you're desperate to get started. Startups.co.uk founder David Lester once invested in a fast food soup company that despite having fabulous soups failed because, in a bid to keep costs low, it took premises that failed to attract enough passing trade. In his book *Starting your own business – the good, the bad and the unexpected* (Crimson Publishing 2007) David muses that with hindsight it would have been better to wait for a more affordable high street location to come along or, alternatively, widen the target area initially identified in the business plan.

Clare Thommen, Boudiche

When you open a shop that nobody has ever heard of before, unless you take a high street with footfall that most new businesses can't afford, people don't just flock in and queue up to buy no matter how nice your shop looks or how great your stock is. Some days after we launched we had literally zero sales and just wanted to cry.

➡ COMMERCIAL CLASSIFICATION

All commercial property in the UK has a government registered 'nature of use' defined by a commercial property classification.

Before you negotiate the lease or purchase of a property you must check what commercial classification it currently falls under. If the property does not already have the correct classification for a shop you need to get planning permission from your local authority. You must bear in mind that planning consent might not be accepted if the local authority feels the change of classification would not benefit the area.

When making a decision, the local authority will take into consideration factors such as whether there is a need for that type of business in the area, traffic and parking requirements, likely causes of nuisance such as noise, smells or environmental hazards the business may cause, trading hours and objections from other occupiers and residents.

There are five commercial classifications and shops, hairdressing salons, post offices and travel agents all fall under A1, except for shops offering 'the sale of food or drink for consumption on the premises or of hot food for consumption off the premises' which are grouped in A3 with cafes. Here's the full classification description for A1 properties:

Class A1. Shops

Use for all or any of the following purposes:

(a) for the retail sale of goods other than hot food
(b) as a post office
(c) for the sale of tickets or as a travel agency
(d) for the sale of sandwiches or other cold food for consumption off the premises
(e) for hairdressing
(f) for the direction of funerals
(g) for the display of goods for sale
(h) for the hiring out of domestic or personal goods or articles
(i) for the reception of goods to be washed, cleaned or repaired

Where the sale, display or service is to visiting members of the public.

So, you can look at any A1 (or A3 if you're selling hot food) properties without needing to apply for a classification change. Unless you've found the perfect place under a different classification and have absolutely set your heart on it, we don't recommend you pursue the route of reclassification as it's one filled with potential problems and could cost you a lot of money and time with no guarantees of a successful outcome. It's certainly not impossible, but be prepared for a long, frustrating delay in your plans.

The other advantage of taking over premises already within your commercial classification is that they're far more likely to be fit for purpose. If you take over a building that's already a shop, while you may rework the actual shell of the shopfloor, it's likely you'll have designated rooms for stock, staff, possibly an office and hopefully the premises will come complete with a decent degree of retail security measures already in place. The savings to be made here shouldn't be underestimated.

➡ LEASE OR BUY?

You've two options when searching for premises: to lease or to buy. For many of you there won't actually be a choice because you won't be able to afford to buy. Even if you can, especially in the current climate of declining property prices, it could be smarter to keep your money in your pocket and not saddle your business with a sizeable mortgage.

Even so, buying does have its advantages. You'll have an asset to play with and the freedom to not have to go seeking your landlord's approval every time you make a change.

One consideration should be the current state of the property market. While commercial property tends to withstand fluctuation better than the residential market, retail and office lets are at their lowest levels for 10 years while many landlords have seen 10% sliced off the value of their portfolios over 2008. Basically, it's a far better time to be renting than owning.

Buy

For many budding shop owners, the idea of owning your own property is just too much of a pipe dream. Property is expensive and with so many costs involved in setting up a new business, a mortgage is an extra burden easily avoided.

Ask yourself the following questions before you decide to buy a property. If you can't answer yes to all of them, buying isn't for you.

- Is the shop in the best location you think you can ever afford?
- Do you plan to keep your shop the same size indefinitely?
- Do you have both a sufficient deposit and the budget for a mortgage, or enough cash to purchase the property outright?

If you're in a comfortable enough position to buy your shop premises, then there are several advantages associated with buying a property. The first and most obvious is that you'll own it, have the freedom do with it as you please, and not have to answer to a landlord. Another major advantage with owning your own shop premises is you'll have a major asset, either to secure loans against or think of as an investment.

As with any property purchase, domestic or commercial, you'll need to carry out the appropriate checks before you agree to buy. Bring in a reputable surveyor, get the place checked with the environmental health officer, and find out what your business rates will be. Do as much research on the building and area as physically possible because if something's not right with it once you've got the keys, it won't be easy to just pack up and move on.

Lease

Leasing is far more common than buying, for the simple reason that it gives you more flexibility in both a physical and a financial sense. If you expand more quickly than anticipated, you can move at relatively short-notice provided you negotiated the right kind of contract when you took out the lease. Also, there are a limited number of properties on the market to buy and you'll find your options are far more open when looking for leased property.

A lease can be negotiated for any length of time that you and the landlord agree on but typically will last anywhere between three and 25 years. The landlord will be looking for a reliable tenant that will run a successful business and consequently be able to pay the rent on time. You may be asked to present a business plan and have your own financial history checked up on. If you don't have any trading history then it's not unheard of for the landlord to ask for anything up to a year's rent in advance, so bear this in mind when budgeting.

However, you have just as much right to do your own checks on the landlord. If possible talk to the current or previous tenants. Find out why they're moving on. If their business failed was it because of the location, something wrong with the property, or even as a result of a difficult landlord? These are the kind of things you'll want to know before signing a lease.

That said, the one advantage to the current economic climate is the power could be swinging back to you as a tenant. It's not uncommon for a landlord, especially if they're struggling to fill a space, to give you an incentive to move in. It's all about supply and demand and don't be afraid to fight your corner just because you're a start-up business. See if you can negotiate a period of free rent to help your business establish itself and use the argument that it's in both your favours for that to happen.

> **FROM THE EXPERTS:**
> ## Mike Clare, Dreams plc
>
> Negotiate hard. Even if you have to give guarantees as a new business, use that as a tool for getting them to give you something back in terms of a rent free period. Judge what the landlord is trying to achieve. If it's been empty for a long time convince him he'll lose money every day it stays empty. If he's being greedy let him incentivise you to pay more so he can make the rest of the block pay the same.

If you intend to grow quickly and think you could be moving on within a couple of years it might be worth haggling over flexibility and get out clauses more than rent.

In reality though, in busier locations, without references from your bank manager or a previous commercial landlord and with no trading record, you should expect to pay three months' rent in advance and six months' rent as a deposit. Clearly, that's a tidy sum and so you'll need to include it in your business plan and any applications for borrowing.

It's easy to get burned when it comes to property deals and the best way to protect yourself is to ask all the right questions, get everything agreed in writing and above all, check your contract with a fine toothcomb.

Here's a few tips and things to consider before signing a lease:

- What kind of rent are similar businesses in the area being charged, and is yours a fare rate in comparison? The simplest way to find out is to ask: you'll find most traders will be just as interested to know if they're overpaying the current asking rate so will be happy to play ball.
- Is the length of lease suitable? If it's too short your shop will lack security but if it's too long and you don't have a break clause, you may find yourself stuck.
- Is the building sound and in a state of good repair? It's advisable to bring in expert help to check there are no serious faults.
- Will the landlord offer a rent-free period if there are repairs to be carried out?
- Do you need planning permission before you can build or alter the shop according to your designs?
- Who is responsible for insurance? What's included in the rent, and what cover will the landlord expect you to take out yourself in addition?

This is by no means an extensive list of everything you should check before signing a contract. It's always advisable to have a solicitor or property expert to check over the small print for you.

How much will it cost?

As you'd expect, prices for buy and leasing vary immensely depending on what it is you're buying and where you're buying, both geographically across the UK and in terms of location within a region.

If you're looking to buy your shop's premises the price will also vary massively depending on whether you're buying just the bricks and mortar or the actual business itself. To get a good idea of prices, search for the kind of shop you're looking to own on either Daltonsweekly.com or businessesforsale.com which both specialise in advertising shops for sale.

The one consistent aspect to lease pricing is that it tends to be measured per square foot. That rate, of course, varies greatly. One property company estimated the average price for shop space on London's Oxford Street in the first half of 2008 at a whopping £530 sq ft, but also revealed you could pay as little as £35 sq ft several miles away in the less affluent or visited Tottenham Hale.

Research by property advisors King Sturge showed Zone A retail space in Birmingham and Leeds to be priced at £300 and £310 respectively, and out-of-town to be £65 and £37 respectively.

While out of town retail parks tend to have lower rates than Zone A locations they offer very few premises for small companies. Indoor shopping centres tend to be slightly lower priced than prime Zone A locations but substantially more than stock in the suburbs. Bluewater and Lakeside which service shoppers from within the M25 are some of the most expensive locations outside of London's Zone A streets.

➡ PROFESSIONAL ADVISORS

Estate agents and commercial property agents

Using estate agents is rarely avoidable, but look to turn it to your advantage by getting them working for you as much as their clients. Be strong minded and clear about what you want and remind them they need you to take the property just as much as they need to sell or fill it for the landlord.

Likewise, consider using a commercial property agent or service who'll actively seek retail space for you and negotiate the best deal. This won't come cheap but you could save what you spend by hiring the services of someone whose ear is close to the ground within the commercial

> ### ✦ TIP
> Use the internet but get as many agents as you can aware of the type of property you require: you want to be at the forefront of their mind the minute they get the perfect property on their books.

property market and has firm contacts with landlords and developers. It's likely they'll also be able to help you with solicitors, builders and architects who they've worked with before. If you do go down this route, pick one who has experience in securing premises for start-up and small businesses and ideally the type of retail trade you're looking to enter.

Solicitors

Getting the right help on board is essential. It's better to have someone steering you clear of problems rather than hiring them to put out fires further down the line. As mentioned, it's really not advisable to sign any contract without it being looked over by an independent legal expert in the property sector.

TIP
To find a specialised solicitor try The Law Society. You can search by location or sector at www.lawsociety.org.uk

If possible, get someone on board who specialises in the shop trade. If they've overseen countless shop sales and leases in the past, the chances are they'll spot any problems or concerns with your deal a mile away.

Builders and architects

Choosing an architect or builder that comes highly recommended is the best way to find someone trustworthy and capable of doing a satisfactory job. Go through organisations such as the Federation of Master Builders (www.fmb.org.uk). Ask friends or other shop owners for advice, or ask for examples of previous work so you can see for yourself what the finished results look like.

You may not be an expert when it comes to building terms, how long things take or how much it's all likely to cost, but it's up to you to do your research and arm yourself with as much knowledge as possible. The more you know, the less likely you are to be taken advantage of.

If you find a builder you like, treat them well because they could come in very useful. Ask questions and don't be embarrassed to ask them to explain something you don't understand. You'll soon find the value to having a basic understanding of what's what when you get quotes.

Before you sign a lease or agree to a mortgage, make sure you've considered all of the following:

- Have other shops been successful in the premises? If not, why? Can you succeed where they've failed?
- Is it the right size? Can you fit as many shelves/display cases as you want?
- Is the property security friendly? Is it easy to break into? Does it have a burglar alarm, and if not, how much would it cost to add one?
- Is it protected against pests such as insects or rodents? Is there somewhere to dispose of waste without attracting unwanted visitors?
- Are there any major structural problems or damaged areas?
- How much are you likely to pay in business rates?
- Are you really certain it's the best possible place for you to locate your shop?

Things to remember:

- Consider your property needs carefully before you even start viewing properties. You need a clear idea of exactly what you require before speaking to agents.

- Weigh up the different options for locations.

- Remember to check the commercial classification of any property you're interested in.

- Don't rush into buying if leasing is more suited to your finances.

- Find a solicitor and estate agent you feel comfortable with.

Decking it out

Y ou've signed the lease and collected the keys, but what next? Now comes the exciting but gruelling task of getting your shop ready to open. Whether you've inherited an existing retail unit that simply needs a lick of paint and rebrand or you're starting from scratch, this chapter will take you through everything from choosing your signage to buying and till and dealing with the utility companies.

Again there are some vital matters you need to consider before you start choosing your colour scheme. Issues such as environmental health requirements and utilities are covered here as well as advice on designing the optimum layout for your shop.

In this chapter we'll cover:

- Things to consider before you start
- Dealing with contractors
- Layout
- Décor and interior
- Signage
- Equipment

➡ BEFORE YOU PICK UP A PAINTBRUSH . . .

Your best planning skills are needed for this stage of the setting up process. Every aspect of the shop's physical appearance and functionality has to be thought out before you start drilling into walls or putting up signs and product displays.

Start with the practical stuff. Sure, kitting out the shop in your ideal colour tone and getting those nice shelves and fancy lights you've eyed might be something you've waited for but make sure your shell is fit for purpose first so you don't have to undo any aesthetic work.

Utilities

Another area to think through carefully is utilities. It's tempting to leave things as they are if the premises already has gas and electricity set up, but the current suppliers may not be the most cost-effective for your business. Shop around using energy and utility switch specialists to get the best deal. A few hours invested in comparing gas and electricity prices may save you a considerable amount in the long-run. Also, if it's a key part of your identity, consider the benefits for switching to a more eco-friendly supplier.

Find out from your landlord or the previous premises owner what the situation is for running water, gas and electricity before you get the keys. You won't be able to do much without working utilities and it may be something you can sort out before the handover of the shop.

> ### IN MY EXPERIENCE:
> ## Paul Mather, Sherston Post Office Stores
>
> Our annual electricity bill is around £4,500 I managed to reduce it by around £500 after using the website Makeitcheaper.com to switch from Scottish Power to Electricity4Business.

DIY or contractors?

Your business plan should have already helped you decide whether or not you'll be doing a DIY job or hiring professional decorators, architects or builders. Even if you decide to do the work yourself, it's a good idea to get some professional advice before you start as they may point out some issues you hadn't considered.

If you decide to bring in contractors you need to have thought about the following before choosing who you want to build your shop:

- The kind of atmosphere you want to achieve
- The colour scheme/design theme you're leaning towards
- The layout of both shopfloor and backend of your premises
- Any specific fittings such as counters, display units and shelving, fitting rooms etc
- The price you're prepared to pay

You need to have thought all of the above through before the first contractor walks through the door so that you can give them a true idea of what they need to offer you, and to avoid being taken advantage of. Don't accept the first price and package you're offered. Get as many different quotations and pitches as time will allow for then compare them before you make a decision. Make sure all quotes are broken down by section, materials and labour: this will give you far more scope for understanding where the real costs are and give you a stronger position to negotiate from.

The last thing you need is trouble with your builders or designers, as this is the most likely cause of a delay in opening or going over budget. For extra reassurance it's worth going via trade bodies such as the Federation of Master Builders. It may cost more, but at least then you can be more confident of a professional service.

Keeping costs down

That said, a massive priority in this stage should be too keep costs down. If a high quality finish as absolutely paramount to your shop's identity then you can just about justify spending heavily on fitting it out. Otherwise, keep it simple and keep the cash in the business.

> **FROM THE EXPERTS:**
> **Mike Clare, Dreams**
>
> Don't use shopfitters, they'll only try and rip you off. Unless you've the type of proposition that needs high quality decor, just concentrate on doing the outside of the shop to pull people in and get open. You can improve the inside later.

Much higher priority than fancy fittings most customers won't value should be expanding your stock range and hitting the level of value (and profit) you've set out in your business plan. You can always refurnish later once the money is swilling in.

> **IN MY EXPERIENCE:**
> **Paul Mather, Sherston Post Office Stores**
>
> A good shopfitter is the key and after getting lots of quotes we struck gold with one who had worked on a similar size shop in the area. He listened, gave advice and played a valuable role in the project.

Timing

Unfortunately delays are common when it comes to getting a shop ready for launch. When planning your opening you might want to consider budgeting in time for unexpected delays. Of course, you can't foresee every problem, but preparing yourself for the odd setback can take some of the pressure off if you do run into roadblocks.

Never pay up front. You should be incentivising your contractors to finish on time; ie they get a chunk upfront, the rest on completion by a non-negotiable deadline – put it in writing that you won't pay for work that's completed after this deadline but that you still expect it to be completed.

➡ SHOP LAYOUT

The basic components of most shops are: shopfloor, stockroom, basic staff area and facilities, small office. That should pretty much be the order of priority as well. Be sensible about your minimum requirements for the rest but make sure you maximise shopfloor space. It's a simple equation: the more space you've got on the shopfloor the more people you can fit in the shop.

You'll also want to leave plenty of space for access. People avoid going into crowded shops, while you'll want to enable access for pushchairs and wheelchairs.

Think about where you'll position the key elements of the shop. Position your counter where you can view as much of the shop as possible – almost always that will be against a back or side wall. Avoid using up window space as this will limit your window displays and the back of the counter area may be visible from the outside.

If you're running a newsagents or convenience store where window display is slightly less valuable and shoplifting of small items common, you'll want to be near the door so customers (and thieves) have to pass you on their way out.

If you require fitting rooms make sure they're at the back of the shop so customers have to walk past all your stock to get to them. Similarly think about how you'll display items when ordering units. Retail positioning and display is a skill and industry in itself. Visit competitors and also large high street stores to study how they carefully position different products to entice the customer in, encourage

> ### ⭐ TIP
>
> You'll want to avoid cluttering the front of the shop with high displays and obscuring stock at the back, so think about this before ordering any units.

at-counter sales and compartmentalise different areas of shops or brands.

Think about the customer experience and what is most likely to encourage them to firstly browse and secondly buy. If you identified in your customer outline and identity that they expect a no frills, streamlined service then that's what they expect to see from your shop. If your customer sees your items as occasional luxury purchases then they'll expect more relaxed and pleasant surroundings in which to make that decision.

Stock room and staff areas

Unless you've particular requirements such as refrigeration needs, you'll want to keep this as simple as possible. Be aware of health and safety and fire regulations but try and use shelving to maximise space. Where possible, use basements.

Ideally though, you'll want to limit the amount of space used to store stock by managing your deliveries economically so you're carrying as little as possible that's not out the front: that said, make sure you've enough as there's nothing worse than sending a customer away disappointed and empty handed.

For staff areas, again, be sensible and don't spend a lot. While your sales assistants might like the idea of a boudoir to pamper themselves in, the reality is they'd prefer to have a job more and that depends on the profitability of your business. Somewhere to store their bags and coats, a fridge to store food, a few seats to sit down for a break and possibly eat and a toilet is all should be all you need.

IN MY EXPERIENCE:
Clare Thommen, Boudiche

We nearly made the huge mistake of leaving ourselves a tiny stock room, but at the last minute made the decision to lose two foot of fitting space and it was the best decision we've ever made. To run a shop you need storage!

➡ DESIGN AND COLOUR

As we've already mentioned, how much time, effort and money you spend on the design concept for your shop should be determined by its identity and the type of customer you've outlined. In the same way you choose what items to sell against this criterion, you'll need to consider how to create an environment that's aligned to it as well.

No matter what type of shop you're opening, you should consider design. It's your job to provide an environment and atmosphere that meets your customers' expectations, that communicates your brand and encourages them to relax.

When you're working on branding and logos you should also be considering the colour and design themes of the store. If you've left this too late, perhaps consider asking whoever did your logo to give you some brand rules about how it can and should ideally be applied to the shop.

✦ TIP

If you're short on ideas or money, take the property-development-TV show gospel of playing it safe with whites, creams and neutral tones and decor.

That said, the most important aspect of design and use of colour is to create the desired atmosphere. In addition, light colour and mirroring can be used to accentuate space and light.

Stick to your brand and customer knowledge. You're not decorating your home remember, this is a public space and it's more important the design works for your customers than you.

IN MY EXPERIENCE:

Clare Thommen, Boudiche

We used an interior designer instead of shopfitter, sourced furniture from eBay, a reclamation fireplace and even lamps from TK Maxx! But in the end it looked stunning.

Signage

Hopefully when you were picking the name for your shop you gave a second or two's thought to what it would look like above the door – or from across the road. Or from a hanging sign as you're approaching from the same side. Or on a board outside the shop . . . If you didn't, well you'd better start now because your signs are a massively important tool for getting people in through the door.

There are no shortage of suppliers who'll make you a sign and facia in any combination of materials and colours from hand painted on wood to blazing neon. You should have three priorities:

- Something simple, bold and clear
- A style that fits your shop design, business identity and customers' tastes
- A sensible price

The first two should be made out into a brief that you present to several suppliers and ask to see designs and quotes for. If they suggest you use certain materials, then ask to see examples of other work they've done using those materials. If you're very clear about what you want, find an example from another shop, take some photos and provide them with your brief.

Signs are important. You've got to be seen. Make it big and bold so long as that doesn't go against your brand and use projecting signs to ensure you're seen from the side. Use balloons or awnings, anything to make you seen. If the council don't like it, keep doing it until they tell you stop, then do it again.

And while signage is important, again, be prudent. You can always redo them when the business is stabilised. There's a chance you'll also want to rebrand or change your design or focus a little if things don't work out as you'd expected, so bear all this in mind before you go spending a fortune you'll later need and regret parting with.

IN MY EXPERIENCE:

Paul Mathers, Sherston Post Office Stores

We made our own brown direction sign and put it up 200 yards from the shop to give cars time to slow down and consider stopping.

Equipment

It's impossible for this book to make you a list of equipment you'll need for your shop. Visit a recognised high street brand and you'll find the minute you walk through the security sensored doors, you're on camera, you'll pass numerous display units containing stock that's often been barcoded at factory status with a system that once scanned at the till automatically brings the price up, deducts that sold item from the stores stock database and, if that triggers a set threshold of remaining stock, prompts the manager to place a new order. If this doesn't register it's probably because your attention has been caught by the flatscreen TV displays or surround sound tunes.

Nip down the road to a florists and, aside from flowers (obviously!) you could find little else than a till, maybe a counter, some buckets and a wrapping dispenser. If you nip next door to a newsagents to get a paper and a chocolate bar you might encounter several refrigeration and freezer units (possibly

TAG Company
Let's find the right solution for you

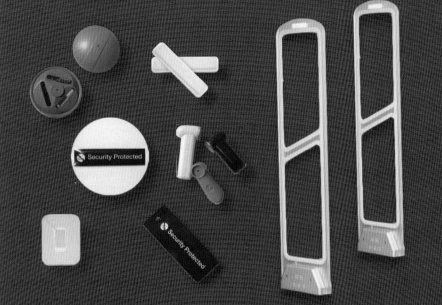

Starting a new business is daunting enough without having to worry about shoplifters. As a new company it is vital to protect your profit. Get the right protection for where you need it with TAG Company: The Tagging Specialist. TAG Company offers you the best EAS (Electronic Article Surveillance) solutions: in both AM and RF frequency. This means together we can determine which one suits your shop best. Most importantly we offer the industry's leading support.

We will offer you a **free quote** after assessing what your needs are. Call us on 0800 781 3598 or visit our website

www.tagcompany.com

TAG
COMPANY

Keep. Track.

branded), cigarette display units, a branded baked products stand, a cash machine, a National Lottery stand, travel ticket machine, electricity and gas key meter charger, maybe even a photocopier.

For want of repeating the same mantra: stick to what your business plan says and the identity decided you needed and don't get tempted by anything else. Think KISS: Keep it simple stupid!

For every purchase ask yourself if you absolutely need it, if your customers would notice if you didn't have it and if you'd definitely only make more money by having it. You'll soon find the nice-to-have luxuries don't pass this test.

Be economical but don't go for the cheapest options on the market. The old adage 'you buy cheap, you buy twice' can certainly ring true when it comes electrical goods and shelving units, and you might end up spending more in the long run if the equipment isn't up to scratch.

That said, buying second hand or leasing equipment is a good way to save money during the early stages of your business without compromising on quality. There are plenty of companies online and in business directories that will lease you with equipment, allowing you to work out what you use most, and what apparatus you think you should return.

Check out retail auctions and discount wholesalers that specialise in selling off stock from business repossessions and liquidations: but don't get tempted to buy just because something is a bargain. If you need it, buy it and do all you can to get the right price. If you don't need it, leave it. If it makes you feel better, make a list of 'phase two' nice-to-have items that you can come back when you've a bit more capital to play with.

IN MY EXPERIENCE:

Clare Thommen, Boudiche

When it's not contributing to the brand, do what you have to. We put in CCTV, stockroom shelving from IKEA, and used an off-the-shelf EPOS system for around £1,500.

OK, so here's a breakdown of the basics almost all of you will require:

Tills

You will need at least one till for your shop depending on its size and scale of operation. Smaller establishments can get away with a basic system while more complicated operations will want to go with a more advanced electronic point of sale (EPOS) system. This is another area where you can choose to either lease or buy.

The more sophisticated EPOS systems will have computerised touch screens which can keep track of exactly what's been ordered and give you accurate up-to-date figures on what your best-selling products are. However the cost of these can run into the thousands and you may find that a standalone system which provides paper printouts is more than adequate for your operation.

For details on how to apply for merchant status to receive credit card payments see the Getting legal chapter.

Shelving and units

Like football referees, the sign that a retail display unit is doing its job well is when you don't notice it. People come to look at the items you're selling, not the shelves they're sitting on. Consequently, the key to buying shelving and units is to decide how you want to set out your shop floor and display your goods.

KISS applies again. As does a fair degree of logic. Think about your experiences as a shopper. You probably prefer shops with space, where you can easily view and sort through items and where products are clearly showcased and demonstrated.

When buying, know what you want and seek the best price. Again look at clearance and auction stock and avoid splashing cash on shiny units that look impressive in catalogues but which you won't be able to see when your product is on them.

Ideally, buy lightweight flexible units that allow you to easily move them around and reorganise the shopfloor in order to keep it fresh and exciting.

IN MY EXPERIENCE:

Paul Mathers, Sherston Post Office Stores

Our sole objective was to increase our limited floor space. We had only 450 sq ft but with clever fittings we increased our selling capacity by a third within the same space.

Counters

The counter is a focal point of the customer experience so although you don't want to go blowing money on something that's effectively a table with an extra side, you should think carefully about your requirements in terms of size, design and what you'll need to fit and display on it.

The counter takes up a sizeable percentage of your shopfloor and is possibly where people will stop and focus most, that's why it's important to consider where it will go when planning your initial shop layout and also include it in your design and colour schemes. As such, it needs meet the all the criterion of your identity etc, but beyond that it also needs to function correctly.

Depending on what type of shop you're running you might need your counter to:

- Display other sales items
- Almost certainly contain one or more tills and point of sale equipment
- Have room for folding and/or packaging items
- Have space to clearly display your payment options and refund policy
- Promote special offers or membership schemes
- Accommodate numerous sales people

Once you've mapped what you need it's a case of deciding if you can buy a readymade product or you'll need a bespoke solution. If you're using an experienced shopfitter it's likely they've come across a wide variety of solutions and should be able to advise the best option as well as building something themselves. Where possible, visit a supplier to see samples.

IN MY EXPERIENCE:

Paul Mather, Sherston Post Office Stores

The best selling space by far is on the counter. Previously chocolate was behind the counter and people had to ask for it, presenting an obvious barrier. Our prime impulse buys are now given prime access.

Security

Before buying anything to secure your shop, make a safety assessment. It might help to get hold of some crime statistics to help you see what types of shop are most prone to different crimes and also consult your insurance provider to see what is worth spending money on in order to keep your premiums down.

If you think shoplifting or theft is likely to be a major problem look at the various measures you can take to prevent it. It could be that you decide to tag individual items with an alarmed security advice, install CCTV, or have a direct emergency alert to the police. If you're selling high value electrical goods, jewellery or clothing it could be worth investing in lockable and alarmed display units or alarm chains and could well require a large safe for overnight storage.

Speak to neighbouring commercial properties about the frequency and propensity of burglary and vandalism and judge what physical security you apply accordingly. Whether other shops have metal rollers on the front is usually a good indication of whether you should – and don't forget to protect the back of the shop as well. All windows should be barred and office and stock room and office areas fitted with secure fire doors.

Always invest in an alarm system and ideally you should have a direct link to the authorities, even if it does mean that nine out of 10 times you're called in the middle of the night because a fox has knocked over a bin or a drunk has pushed against the door.

> ### FROM THE EXPERTS:
> ### John Spooner, Monsoon
>
> Don't spend more than you can lose. If you're selling Rolex watches then yes get close circuit television or a tagging system, but don't do it for the sake of it. Better to wait three months and see what crime is costing you.

Packaging and bags

Five years ago this section would have simply been labelled 'plastic bags' with the discussion being what quality, plain or emblazoned with a logo, and whether you should charge or not. Those considerations are all still valid, but in today's eco-aware society you should also be exploring alternatives to plastic bags.

Bags for life and cotton, jute and canvas bags are increasingly popular, while paper, obviously recycled, has made a comeback ahead of plastic.

However, customers often relish goods that come with luxurious and well designed bags they'll use again regardless of the material they're made from, especially if you're a fashionable or desirable brand.

Bags are potentially a great marketing tool, with customers potentially carrying your brand, website address, phone number etc past more people than you could ever reach with a very significant marketing budget. However, remember it's not free publicity either so factor the additional cost of branded packaging into your marketing budget.

Also consider the customer's perspective. It might make marketing sense to have great looking plastic bags, but you could be on rocky ground if your customer considers it an unnecessary expense and would have preferred a simpler packaged, lower priced purchase. Additionally, should you return cap in hand for another loan, expect the bank to argue the same.

IN MY EXPERIENCE:

Clare Thommen, Boudiche

Sending our customer away with a beautiful hand wrapped package is a crucial part of brand experience, but it rightly wouldn't be a sensible spend for other businesses.

Air conditioning

It's a luxury some need and everyone would like. If you need it to keep products chilled then don't scrimp because if it fails, you won't just be feeling the heat for day or so but be left without income and with a whole pile of wasted stock.

Increasingly, air conditioning is seen as essential to providing a buying environment and attracting passers-by off the streets and into your shop. It's your call but remember you can add it later.

IN MY EXPERIENCE:

Lance Prebble, Pole Position

If you're selling a product people are passionate about the chances are they won't care if your shop is roasting hot, but if you're talking about impulse buyers you need to do everything you can to make them comfortable.

Things to remember:

- Check your utilities are due to work before you move in. You may arrive to a gasless, electricity free property.

- Work out your timings to ensure everything gets finished on time.

- Don't be tempted to decorate solely to your taste. It's the customer's experience that should be at the forefront of your mind.

- Consider leasing equipment as a way to free up cashflow during your first few months.

Getting legal

Running a business today involves adhering to a multitude of laws and regulations, and shops are certainly no exception. Indeed, shops have the potential to be affected by a whole host of restrictions. Working directly with the public, taking payments and welcoming people onto your premises always has legal implications. Employing people is a legal minefield and retail traditionally sees a high turnover of staff. The items you sell might well be liable to certain restrictions or licenses, while you'll need to ensure you manage deliveries, waste disposal and property upkeep within legal and local council jurisdiction.

While other areas such as cashflow, planning and PR make your business, failing to stay inside the law – no matter how tedious it feels – can break it. We'll guide you through everything you need to consider to ensure you're fully compliant. In addition you'll have to manage all the legal responsibilities faced by all businesses.

In this chapter we'll cover:

- Taking money
- Your obligations as a shop owner, employer and business owner
- Licensing
- Health and safety
- Insurance

➡ MONEY

Credit cards

If you're thinking of not taking debit or credit card payments, think again. Sure there are still small shops that get by only accepting cash and cheques and, yes, it will cost you money to take card payments, but customers choosing to shop with you should be worth that cost. As a new business, you simply can't afford not to take payment by card. If you're genuinely worried about the cost, factor for taking 50% of your payments this way into your pricing strategy. Don't make the mistake of charging extra for paying by card either, this will only act as a disincentive for purchase.

High levels of fraud means credit card companies use various methods to ensure illegal activity is kept to a minimum. One is chargebacks, which means if a payment is found to be fraudulent, the credit card company hold you liable for the money it repays to the cardholder. This can occur up to six months after the transaction has taken place and it falls to you to recover the fraudulent funds. As a result you'll need to ensure you take adequate measures to prevent this happening.

> ### ✦ TIP
> Getting merchant status is necessary if you want to accept credit and debit card payments in your shop. You no longer need to have a trading history to apply for merchant status but you will be subject to stringent checks and acceptance isn't automatic.

The process of applying for merchant status involves getting in touch with your bank. The main high street banks offer more or less the same uniform services. The process takes about a fortnight and if you have no trading history it's likely you will be asked to provide your business plan. Longer established shops will generally have to produce around three years' worth of accounts. If you plan to take any orders over the phone you'll need to state this at the time of applying, as 'customer not present' transactions require special permission.

In terms of price, it's a good idea to shop around if you are willing to look further afield than your business bank account provider. Most of the main banks charge roughly 3% per transaction, £15–£25 per month for the rental of the swipe machine and a one-off set up fee of £100–£150.

That's the average cost, however it is possible to negotiate these rates so don't be afraid to ask for a lower rate or ask the bank to combine it with the free services they'll almost certainly give you for your first few years of custom.

Notes forgery

Despite the dramatic increase in paying with plastic, note forgery is still prevalent and while rare, fraudsters often see small independent shops without the technology of large stores as the ideal place to pass these notes on. It pays then to educate yourself on how to recognise a fake.

Knowingly accepting fake notes is clearly illegal, however you're also responsible for making sure any cash you accept is genuine. Ignorance is not an excuse so you can't just turn a blind eye if you suspect customers have given you counterfeit money. Banks will not accept fake notes from you so you will lose out financially if you don't apply an adequate level of vigilance in addition to facing possible criminal proceedings.

When checking for fake notes, don't just rely on one method. Feel the notes in your hands and if in doubt, compare with one you know is genuine. The easiest way to check notes are genuine is with an ultra violet pen. The pen causes a chemical reaction between the ink and the paper, but you'll need to replace them regularly as dirty pens can be unreliable. If you don't have any kind of counterfeit detecting device a few elements to compare genuine notes to are:

- The paper and raised print
- The metallic thread
- The watermark
- The print quality
- The hologram

If you suspect you have received a counterfeit note you must report it to the police immediately. They will then give you a receipt and send it to the Bank of England (Threadneedle Street, London EC2R 8AH). If it turns out to be genuine, they will refund you.

➡ SALE OF ITEMS

When customers buy or hire goods from your shop you are entering into a legally binding contract with them that gives them certain key legal rights. The rights are governed by the Sale of Goods Act 1979 and monitored by Trading Standards.

Some shops stick to the basic legal rights of a consumer, others provide extra options as a way of providing a greater level of customer service. You'll need to understand the law in order to know what you have to offer and decide what else you'll include in your contract of sale.

What you need to know

Legally, all goods, products and services you sell must 'match the description' you give of them. If you say a TV has a 42£ screen then it must have a 42£ screen, if you sell 'homemade' pies they must be homemade. If you claim your products are made from recycled material, they must be. If you don't ensure this customers will be entitled to a full refund and you could face legal action.

Goods must also be of 'satisfactory quality' that a 'reasonable person' would be able consume, use, work properly, and have no defects in their appearance or finish.

Similarly, goods must 'be fit for the purpose specified'. A camera should take photographs and a watch should tell the time. If the items are not suitable to use in certain conditions, such as in water or direct sunlight, they should say so.

Customer's rights

By law, the customer has these rights against you, the supplier of these goods and not the manufacturer. In some cases, the goods may be covered by a manufacturer's guarantee, meaning the manufacturer will repair an item free of charge but it'll be up to you to stipulate this and it won't affect a customer's rights against you as a supplier.

Also, consumers are protected from unfair treatment by traders. You are prohibited from using unfair commercial practices that are misleading or aggressive or omit or hide key information that a consumer might need to make a free and informed purchasing decision.

It's also an offence to display signs that state or imply a consumer, with a genuine complaint, would not be entitled to a refund. For some reason, plenty of shops think it is fine to flout the law providing they advertise the fact they intend to. Examples of statements which the courts have deemed illegal are as follows:

- 'No Cash Refunds'
- 'No Sale Goods Exchanged or Money Refunded'
- 'Sold as Seen and Inspected'
- 'Please Examine Your Goods with Care Because our Liability Ends Once they Leave the Premises'
- 'No Refunds or Exchanges Without a Receipt'

The point where you enter into a contract with a consumer is when you accept their purchase and take their money. You're not obligated to accept that offer and enter into a contract at any point. The most common misconception surrounding this area is that if you offer an item for sale at a certain price you must accept a sale.

This often proves a problem when an item is mispriced by mistake. Because of confusion over the law, some shoppers will claim you must accept £4.40 for an item that was meant to be priced at £44 under 'trading standards'. You don't. By displaying an item for sale, at any price, you're merely offering, in legal speak, 'an invitation to treat' and asking the consumer to make an offer at that price. You're completely entitled to reject that offer providing you've not deliberately mislead them.

Refunds

Once you've accepted an offer and entered into a contract with a consumer you'll be obligated to offer a refund for circumstances where you've legally breached your obligations. This is where it becomes a personal policy of the shop and a complicated issue. Some shops offer refunds above and beyond what is legally required, which while providing a superior service to their customers had clouded the consumer perspective of what they're legally entitled to. In turn, there are also some outlawed return practices commonly occurring on high street shops because either the shop owners don't understand the law or they are prepared to take the risk of flouting it.

The law itself is actually quite simple. Providing proof of purchase (receipt, bank statement or credit card evidence) is provided, you must give a full refund if goods aren't of satisfactory quality or fit for purpose. The consumer maintains these rights even if the item was discounted or sold in a sale. The exception to this is if an item has been labelled as faulty and is being returned for that reason. An item still qualifies for a refund if it is purchased with a fault but proves not fit for purpose or unsatisfactory for another reason.

> **TIP**
>
> You are not legally entitled to give a refund or to exchange goods for any other reason. If someone returns an item to your shop simply because they've changed their mind, say they were bought it as a present, the item doesn't fit, they don't like the colour or any other reason, you don't have to do anything.

That said, it's often in your favour to do so. Consumers' expectations of a genuine reason for returning or exchanging an item is very different to the laws and it's up to you how far you meet that. You should consider that so long as the returned item is fit for resale, it's better to have a happy customer likely to make return purchases and tell others about your excellent customer service than one sale and someone spreading a negative experience of shopping with you. Clearly though, there's a balance to be struck here and you shouldn't take stock back that you can't resell.

IN MY EXPERIENCE:
Lance Prebble, Pole Position

I don't legally have to give people refunds a lot of the time, but sometimes it's better to swallow it if they're a screamer because you don't want the bad word of mouth or to stand arguing with a customer.

Loss or damage in transit

One exception to the point of liability in your contract with the consumer is where you agree to dispatch and deliver items. Despite having completed a financial transaction, the goods remain your liability until delivered.

Therefore it's your responsibility to ensure that goods are not lost or damaged in transit and that you take out the appropriate insurance.

Licences and further regulations

Depending on what type of business you're opening and the kind of products you will be selling, you might require a licence in order to trade. Even you don't need to obtain an actual licence, you might need to adhere to a licensing law.

There are too many licensing requirements for to list here so you should seek advice if you think this might apply to you. The Business Link website has an interactive tool which helps you search for licenses applicable to your shop.

Go to www.businesslink.gov.uk click on Starting Up on the right hand side and then on 'Create a personalised list of licences and permits needed by your business' in the Tools section.

One of the more common licensing requirements surrounds the sale of alcohol. The Licensing Act 2003, which came into force in England and Wales in November 2005, requires businesses to have a licence if they wish to sell or supply alcohol.

Under the new system, you no longer apply to the magistrate's court for your local licence but to your local authority. You'll need to apply for a personal licence in order to issue or authorise the sale of alcohol and also a premises licence to sell from your shop.

The process sees you acquire the necessary forms from your local council, first apply for a personal license, wait for clearance, then a premises licence which involves detailing your operating hours and practises and meeting safety and responsibility criteria, then nominating a premises supervisor who remains the main point of contact. You must then advertise your Notice of Application for Grant of Premises Licence on a nearby lamp post for 28 days and in a local paper before your licence is finally granted.

TIP

The licence process is likely to take up to four months from start to finish and while charges vary by region average costs are around £900. A premises licence lasts for the life of the business at that location and a personal licence lasts for 10 years. You'll be expected to pay an annual licence fee to your local authority in the region of £350.

Audio licence

Another licensing requirement you're likely to encounter is the need for a licence if you want to play music in your shop. It might sound onerous but officially to use copyrighted music in the background of any public setting you need a licence from the Performing Rights Society (PRS), and if the music is pre-recorded, you will also need a Phonographic Performance Limited licence.

Waste Electrical and Electronic Equipment (WEEE) Regulations

If you intend to sell electrical goods in your shop, you're obligated to provide your customers with information on the Waste Electrical and Electronic Equipment (WEEE) regulations.

You must provide your customers with information on:

- The environmental impacts of the substances in EEE and waste electrical and electronic equipment (WEEE)
- The reasons for separating WEEE from other waste
- The meaning of the crossed out wheeled bin symbol
- How they can safely dispose of WEEE for proper treatment and recycling free of charge

You must also keep evidence for four years that you have provided this information, but not information on individual cases. You must display information to customers on the benefits of take-back schemes through posters or leaflets.

For more information, visit: www.netregs.gov.uk

Smoking

In July 2007, a smoking ban was introduced in England, having already been established in Scotland, Wales and Northern Ireland. The ban made smoking in all enclosed public spaces and workplaces illegal.

Under no circumstances can you allow customers or staff to smoke inside your shop. The smoking ban also extends to any company vehicles used by more than one person, regardless of whether there's more than one person in the vehicle at the time. The ban is enforced by local authorities and failure to adhere to it carries a fine of up to £2,500.

Health and safety

As your shop involves inviting members of the public onto your premises, and quite possibly staff, you're legally obliged to provide adequate health and safety practises. This can involve a lot of tedious paper work, and laborious training, but unfortunately there's just no getting away from it.

You are responsible for the wellbeing of every single person that visits your shop:

- Staff
- Customers
- Anyone else from the delivery people to plumbers and friends

Shops aren't as dangerous as many other business environments such as factories or restaurant kitchens, but that doesn't mean there aren't special considerations you'll need to pre-empt. Carrying stock, heavy lifting and using instruments such as scalpels to open boxes can expose staff to injury and as an employer it's your legal obligation to ensure you take all necessary measures to avoid this happening.

You should:

- Record and report all accidents
- Consult all staff on health and safety measures
- Ensure staff are aware of health and safety procedures and comply with them

Your local authority and the Health and Safety Executive (HSE) are the governing bodies that make sure you are meeting your obligations. However, they are not just there to enforce and punish you when you make a mistake. You can also ask their advice and even invite them to your shop premises to help you with your risk assessment and safety procedures.

TIP

For more information on health and safety and how to carry out a risk assessment of your business you can visit the HSE website at www.hse.gov.uk.

Accessibility

Under the Disability Discrimination Act you must also take all 'reasonable steps' to ensure your shop has no physical barriers that prevent disabled people from accessing it. This covers any 'physical features' such as steps, heavy doors, insufficient lighting, lack of signs and poor colour contrast. Failure to do so could result in a hefty fine but more importantly you could be missing out on custom from the UK's 10 million disabled shoppers.

Waste disposal

Your shop will generate waste and you need to be aware of your legal responsibilities regarding its disposal. The law requires you to keep all waste tidy and safe. This means ensuring there is a specific area, away from the public where waste can be stored securely, and hygienically, until it's removed.

Under the Environment Protection Act 1990 you must:

- Arrange a trade waste collection agreement with the local authority or an authorised licensed waste carrier (note: your business rates do not include payment for waste disposal)
- Keep records on the type of waste you give to the collector
- Only put waste out on the street on the day of collection and in proper waste containers so it's contained
- Not, under any circumstances, put commercial waste into litterbins or try to dispose of it via domestic waste collections

Failure to comply with these requirements could result in a fixed penalty notice or a court appearance. These requirements can also vary from region to region, so contact your local council to ensure you're operating within the law.

IN MY EXPERIENCE:

Lance Prebble, Pole Position

Waste is an extra bill you expect to be covered by your rates. I have to pay £1 for a bag that's got City of Westminster printed on it and the same for sticky tape to be able to leave cardboard outside. Look into the costs with your local council.

Fire safety

The laws surrounding businesses and their fire safety requirements have undergone significant reform in recent years. The Regulatory Reform (Fire Safety) Order 2005 came into force across England and Wales in October 2006.

The order places emphasis towards risk reduction and fire prevention and means that fire certificates are no longer issued. Instead, you must carry out a fire risk assessment for your premises. The assessment should pay particular attention to those at special risk, such as young people, the disabled and those with special needs. You will also need to produce an emergency plan.

Your local fire authority can give you more details on how to carry out the fire risk assessment and what details you need to include in your emergency plan.

➡ INSURANCE

As you're yet to open the doors to your shop, it's unlikely you've much enthusiasm for thinking about all the things that could go wrong. However, while it's not the sexiest element of starting-up, ensuring your business has the necessary insurance cover will protect all the hard work you're putting in elsewhere.

Some insurance cover is required by law, others make total business sense even though they seem an expensive overhead to take on when first starting out. Instead of looking at what insurance will cost you now, you should consider the implications of a disaster on your business.

Employers' Liability Insurance (ELI)

If you employ one other member of staff you are required by law to have this cover or you could face a fine. This type of insurance helps you meet the cost of compensation for staff if they are injured while working. Policies generally start at around £10m worth of cover to include legal expenses. However, ELI doesn't mean you're untouchable. You must still honour all your health and safety obligations, carry out regular risk assessments and have all the appropriate paperwork to back this up. To find out more about your health and safety obligations visit the HSE website: www.hse.gov.uk

Product and public liability insurance

Although not compulsory by law, as a shop owner you'd be very foolish not to take out this kind of cover, as it will protect you against claims made against your shop by members of the public. As your business relies on members of the public entering your premises, buying and using the goods that you sell, you need to protect yourself should anything untoward happen. However, it's still your responsibility to ensure your premises are safe and your goods meet all the necessary requirements.

Premises insurance

Your shop's chances of survival will be severely compromised if the actual premises are damaged. You can take out cover against damage as a result of any number of unforeseen occurrences such as floods, fires, or malicious damage. Vandalism, unfortunately is common, especially for shops located near nightclubs and pubs where drunken incidents are at their highest. It's also not unknown for vindictive customers or even competitors to cause damage to your shop. Landlords will sometimes cover certain aspects of buildings damage but responsibility for shopfronts will almost certainly remain with you and could prove costly if it's a frequent occurrence. The more measures you take to limit damage, such as CCTV and metal roller shutters, the easier it'll be to keep premiums down.

Contents insurance

As premises insurance only covers the physical building, you'll need to make sure the contents of your shop are also adequately insured against damage or theft. This will cover stock, machinery, shop furniture and anything else included in the policy.

Business interruption insurance

While covering you against the costs of repair and replacement, contents and premises insurance won't necessarily help with any income you lose while your shop is closed as a result of unforeseen events. This is where business interruption insurance comes in.

When the Buncefield oil explosions occurred in December 2005 several companies went out of business overnight. Online fashion retailer ASOS could easily have been one. It lost £3m worth of stock at in its busiest week of the year, cancelled and refunded 19,000 orders and closed the site for six weeks. Fortunately, CEO Nick Robertson had the company insured to the hilt with a firm disaster recovery plan in place. Business interruption insurance covered ASOS for the lost business and included provision for an extensive advertising campaign for relaunch. When the site began trading again in late-January 2006, it took record sales on its first day.

Other insurance

Large insurance companies will offer packages aimed at specifically at shop owners and these are definitely worth looking at. While they might not offer massive savings, they're likely to include valuable extras such as insurance against season increases, inflation, loss of licences, equipment breakdown and legal issues. If you're a partnership you should also look at taking out insurance cover to protect the business should one of the key directors fall ill or, worse still, die.

IN MY EXPERIENCE:

Paul Mather, Sherston Post Office Stores

I've claimed several times for loss of frozen stock caused by prolonged electric cuts; and it's definitely paid to be covered.

Things to remember:

Before opening your doors to customers make sure you've addressed everything on the legal checklist. Have you:

- Got the right insurance?

- Registered with your local authority 28 days before opening?

- Got the right licence under The Licensing Act 2003?

- Made sure your health and safety assessments and procedures are in place and staff are adequately trained?

- Carried out a fire risk assessment?

- Arranged for a collector to dispose of commercial waste?

_2.5_

Buying stock

Y   ou can be the best manager in the world but without good products, you won't get the customers in to buy them. It's precisely for this reason that you need a healthy relationship with the best suppliers you can possibly find. A fine balance must be struck between the products you can afford and the quality you need to meet your customer's expectations.

In this chapter you'll find advice on how to find local suppliers and the advantages this can have for your shop. Maintaining a good relationship with your supplier is vital, and can be beneficial to both parties. However you must also make sure you're using that relationship to the best advantage for your business. We cover using wholesalers, manufacturers and the positives and negatives of buying from abroad.

In this chapter we'll cover:

- Sourcing suppliers
- Sourcing manufacturers at home and abroad
- Dealing with suppliers
- Credit options

➡ STOCKING YOUR SHOP

The great thing about running a shop is, when you strip it down, you're operating an age old business model that's essentially the purest form of capitalism: you're buying something for one price in order to sell it on at a profit. So far though, we've spent a disproportionate amount of time focusing on selling: how you'll attract customers, what's the USP that pulls them in, securing premises they'll want to visit etc. And there's far more to come, how you'll design your shop, display your products, market yourself, build a brand etc.

That's all massively important, of course, but it ignores a rather crucial fact: it doesn't matter how many customers you attract if you can't get hold of the right products at the right price. This applies even if you're manufacturing your own products. Unless you're planning to sell thin air, you'll still need to source the raw materials.

Indeed, the sad truth is, there are just as many businesses that go bust because they don't dedicate time to finding the right suppliers as those that can't find enough customers.

IN MY EXPERIENCE:
Clare Thommen, Boudiche

It's not easy! We had no idea where to start and wasted hours searching the internet. The breakthrough was when we attended a trade fair where all the main suppliers and manufacturers were and we found out about the industry trade magazine, which was a godsend.

➡ WHAT YOU'RE LOOKING TO BUY

Before we start looking for suppliers you need to be confident about what you're looking to buy.

There's a myth, largely among retailers who've lost sight of who they're selling to, that says 'you can never really tell if something is going to sell or not'. This isn't true. You should be pretty damn confident it'll sell if you're parting with your hard earned cash, actually! Traders who use this lame excuse are buying blind because they've lost sight of who their customer is – and that's what should be at the forefront of your mind with every buying purchase.

You've worked hard to outline your target customer in planning your business, now don't lose sight of what they want to buy or get blinded by goods or products that are 'near matches' simply because a supplier is offering it a discounted price. Stick to your guns. Make lists.

Also be careful about how much you buy. When you're first starting out, keep it simple: stick to what you're most confident will sell best and look to diversify and extend the range later on. Buy smaller amounts of stock until you've proven you'll be able to sell it, even it means you don't initially make the same profit you could make by buying in bulk – a small profit is far better than a big loss on stock you wrongly thought would sell.

You should aim for an 80:20 ratio combination of safe selling essential items and unique unusual items. That way, customers will feel assured you'll stock items they need as well as surprises they'll want. For a women's clothes store you'll want 80% of your stock from known designers carrying the latest fashion ranges but to give your store a unique edge over the high street competitors you might use the other 20% to showcase local emerging designers you can sign exclusive deals with. Alternatively, for a convenience store it could be that your unique stock are flowers if there's not a florist in the area or carrying international produce appealing to immigrants populations.

> **FROM THE EXPERTS:**
> **Mike Clare, Dreams**
>
> Put your most unusual stuff in the window as the most popular won't pull people in. People know we sell standard beds, it's the unusual stuff that catches their attention.

➡ SOURCING SUPPLIERS

The type of shop you're opening will largely decide how and where you source your products and goods and the type of suppliers you need to speak to. Mostly though, you'll buy through one of the following ways:

- Wholesaler / cash 'n' carry
- Direct from manufacturers or suppliers
- From abroad / importers

Wholesalers/cash 'n' carry

If you're looking to stock familiar items sold in lots of other shops – and there's nothing wrong with that – then it's unlikely you'll need to do anything other than find your nearest couple of cash 'n' carry outlets. For well known brands, prices won't vary massively outside of special offers so there's little point travelling too far, especially once you factor in the cost of petrol.

Cash 'n' carry outlets

These work in exactly the same way as you but on a larger scale. You'll find it very much like shopping in a supermarket for giants. Everything comes in multipacks and is stocked high. You'll get a large trolley, pick what you want and pay at the till. Remember, prices won't include VAT so you'll need to add on 17.5% when you're working out your profit margins.

Much as when you're looking for value in your weekly supermarket shop, pay special attention to special offers. Discounting stock can give your profits a real boost or you can choose to pass on that discount as an incentive to attract customers. But only buy what's on special offer if you're convinced you can clear it and don't get hooked by a mouth-watering bargain.

Wholesalers

Wholesalers operate in much the same way although you'll find they specialise more in certain types of goods. Like cash 'n' carries they tend to cluster together in industrials areas of cities. In London, for example, most are located to the west near Wembley and Park Royal, making them more accessible for the rest of the country. The centrality of the midlands also makes is a logistical hub for distributors and wholesalers.

> ### ✦ TIP
> Some wholesalers will require you to have a trade or membership card, but don't be put off by this. It's usually something you can fill in at the counter with proof of business status such as bank statement.

Wholesalers are fairly traditional in how they advertise themselves and you're just as likely to track them down in the Yellow Pages as online, however slowly but surely they are beginning to use the web to reveal their whereabouts and even advertise their goods.

TIP

www.thewholesaler.co.uk is the most established site for UK wholesalers. For a cash 'n' carry, visit your nearest Booker, the largest branded wholesaler, for research purposes to get a feel for what's on offer and then see if any smaller independents can better their prices.

Before you set off on a visit, phone ahead to check about the products they've got on offer and in stock and for their best prices. Get the person's name that you speak to so you can find them when you get there. It'll make you seem more experienced and they'll be more inclined to help you find what you're looking for – and maybe even give you a discount.

Negotiation is the norm when it comes to buying in bulk and the wholesale warehouse floor is where the deals are made. The prospect of battling it out with a cockney 'del boy' might terrify some of you but it needn't be anywhere near so scary. Simply open negotiations by asking something such as, 'If I take three batches of this instead of two, are you going to give me x% discount?'

Remember, it's in a wholesaler's favour for you to make a healthy profit to ensure your business prospers and you keep coming back for more stock, so there's always room for negotiation on advertised prices. Obviously, the more you buy the more flexible wholesalers are likely to be. A £200 sale isn't a big deal to them so be realistic. That said, discounts of up to 20% are common place when a deal's there to be struck.

It's also possible to get credit from many wholesalers and even at a cash 'n' carry. The process differs little from applying for any other form of credit and just involves filling out the relevant forms and usually a basic credit check. It's definitely an option many shops take advantage of but you should probably stick to using bank debt to begin with as it's a lot easier to keep control of your finances if they're all in one place. You'll also want to make sure you're happy with a wholesaler's service before you start taking credit from it.

TIP

Most cash 'n' carry outlets and warehouses are open Monday to Friday and for part of Sunday. As inconvenient as it might be, they also tend to close from Christmas Eve through to 2 January.

Direct from manufacturers or suppliers

As opposed to physically visiting a cash 'n' carry or wholesaler and bringing your newly acquired goods back to the shop, you can also buy directly from manufacturers or suppliers who'll deliver to you.

Your decision to buy directly from a manufacturer could be because you specifically want to stock a certain brand or product. If they don't sell through wholesale most large companies will have a department set up to deal with direct sales and distribution and you should look to contact them directly.

Most suppliers welcome any trade and while you might struggle to get credit with them as a start-up, they'll be happy to supply you. Others though, often branded products such as clothing or premium food and drink products, will want to see evidence that your shop's profile fits their brand. They'll either visit you or you'll be expected to go to their premises to pitch to become an official reseller and prove you understand the way they'd like their goods to be sold. Certain brands are deliberately picky and, silly as it might seem, you'll have to work hard to earn the right to sell their goods.

In turn, you'll find it'll work the other way round as well and you'll be approached by sales people asking you to stock their products. As the foot is on the other shoe you should be able to negotiate free or heavily discounted products for your first order to see how well they'll sell.

When buying direct from suppliers or manufacturers you may also be able to negotiate or even be offered a 'sale or return' deal. This means you'll be refunded for any items you don't sell within an agreed period of time. However, most 'sale or return' will see you earn a commission of 10%–20% per unit sold, instead of the larger mark-up you'd expect from buying wholesale. It is a sensible way of testing the market for goods though before risking a large outlay.

Trade fairs

The other way you'll find direct suppliers and manufacturers is through trade fairs. Here companies showcase their products and latest ranges. It's always worth attending the main trade fairs in your industry, even if it's only to keep an eye on emerging trends and new suppliers who might be able to cut you a better deal in order to secure your services. Trade fairs also present the opportunity to find smaller suppliers that otherwise weren't on your radar and pick up something unique. Exhibitions.co.uk is a listings site for the main UK trade fairs but you should also make an effort to find out about industry specific events by reading trade magazines and asking your suppliers which they attend.

When you visit a trade fair, study the website or guidebook before to highlight companies that might be of interest to you and try to be quite strategic about visiting them as a priority. Trade fairs tend to be large maze-like villages of generic exhibition stands and smiling faces handing out plastic bags and sweets making it easy to switch off and miss what you originally went for. Take a dictaphone instead of a trying to make notes you won't be able to read and wear something smart but comfortable – you could be there for hours.

TIP

On the issue of time, make sure you allow plenty of it. You might only attend one trade fair a year but that's your one window to potentially find your five best-selling products so it really is worth booking out the whole day – or even two. If you are there overnight, amend your hitlist for the second day.

Buying from abroad/importers

Why is it attractive to buy from abroad?

There are quite simply huge savings to be had from buying produce from abroad. In fact, it's not just savings, you'll find items that you can't buy anywhere else and which will have a mark-up far in excess of anything you'll buy and sell from a UK manufacturer or wholesaler.

China and India are the booming economies of the world, however, their export trades are very much geared to supplying big business and rarely ship items in smaller amounts than 40ft containers. Smaller amounts are easier to source from countries such as Thailand and Indonesia, specifically Bali, where there's a good variety of product that's very saleable in the UK market. Increasingly, UK shop owners are importing everything from jewellery to clothing and interior design products at rock bottom prices that make it mouth-wateringly tempting.

However, while international trade is becoming far more commonplace among small business owners, it's remains laden in risk for a start-up like you. There are also significant costs to consider that will counter-balance what initially seem like massive mark-ups. In addition to purchase price, factor in the cost of finding suppliers, packing and transportation, insurance and customs duty.

You'll also need to account for a degree of leeway in this, as when you're managing large imports even a slight fluctuation in transport charges or exchange rates can eat massively into your profits.

> **TIP**
>
> Relying completely on goods imported from abroad is a riskier strategy than buying from home simply because there are more factors beyond your direct control.

Finding a supplier abroad

You've two options for finding overseas suppliers, either seek them yourself and buy directly or go indirectly through an importer. Buying directly offers you the greatest mark-up but you'll have to find them, arrange the deal, transportation and maintain all lines of communication on your own. Using an importer is far less risky and taxing but, predictably, the profit you can make is nowhere near as high, while the chance of you importing something truly unique is also less.

If you're thinking of importing directly, the first thing you need to do is find a supplier. You can fly out to the countries you know specialise in your goods on a fact finding trip and go seeking suppliers yourself, much as you might plan an exploratory trip to West London warehouse depots. If you do this, try and plan as much as you can in advance. Research regions that specialise in export supply, look for clusters of suppliers, try and contact UK business networks in that country and ask all your contacts for advice. While expensive it could also be worth taking a translator with you.

A safer and easier way to begin is either by using a supplier recommended via word of mouth from someone who has already successfully imported with them or by consulting trade bodies in your sector who might have a list of recommended international suppliers. Likewise, each country's embassy should have a commercial department. See the Foreign and Commonwealth Office website (www.fco.gov.uk) for more details.

> **TIP**
>
> To ensure you're buying from a legitimate supplier look for a proven track record of supplying goods to the UK, ask for the name of UK customers so you can check this, and ask to speak to the main sales agent you'll be dealing with to ensure there will be no insurmountable language barriers.

Striking a deal and protecting yourself

The key here is to be absolutely clear about what you're buying and for how much. Get it all in a legally binding, bilingual contract and leave nothing unaccounted for. If you can, try to be there or have a representative present when goods are packed or transported. Chances are you'll be fine but there are plenty of horror stories of business owners who sign off and pay up for goods only to see something that bears little resemblance arrive in the UK a month later. If you're in any way suspicious, first question why you're doing the deal. Second, order a small amount as a test.

Don't scrimp on insurance. Get some good advice from an insurance broker on product liability insurance for the goods you're importing, marine insurance (which covers you for all transportation) and look to cover goods for the contract price plus and extra 10% to account for the extra costs you'll incur if something goes wrong.

Transporting goods

Aside from cultural obstacles and the dangers of being ripped-of, the main problem is the unreliability of affordable transportation. Shipping is the cheapest option but involves taking out a container (20ft is usually the smallest, with 40ft standard) that runs the risk of being delayed at both ends or departure and arrival and you simply can't open a shop without stock. The same applies to post items, while sending them by airfreight or loose cargo can be massively expensive as you'll pay by weight.

✦ TIP

By far the best way is to carry items back with you as luggage, but unless you're buying jewellery that can't be carried in substantial quantity with ease there's very little point.

Paying customs tax and legal responsibilities

There are various legal obligations you'll need to comply with depending on what it is you're looking to import.

There are limitations, quotas and special controls governing the import of certain products such as foods, medicinal products, plants, animals, metals and textiles. In some cases you'll require an import license, others you'll need to provide proof of country of origin, while many items are subject to inspection.

You'll also have to pay any duty and VAT that applies to the goods you're importing under UK and EC law before they are released to you. Your freight transporter can sometimes pay this and re-invoice you for it; otherwise you'll need to seek advice from HM Revenues and Customs (HMRC) and an accountant on what you need to pay. Make sure you do this advance so you're clear about the real cost of the goods you're buying.

Is it really worth it?

In brief, while it's massively tempting, for most of you buying from abroad is better put on hold until you've established your business and can survive if an order is massively delayed or, worse still, doesn't arrive at all.

If you do go ahead, be as thorough as you can possibly be. Without doubt you shouldn't buy without flying out and visiting the supplier to see the goods. Indeed, you'll usually only find the best deals by doing this.

> **FROM THE EXPERTS:**
> ## John Spooner, Monsoon
>
> It's likely the minimums for going to China, India, Taiwan etc will be too much for you to begin with and you've got to factor in the cost of controllability for the sake of the extra margin as well. However, there's no doubting if you do your preparation and have budget for this, you'll feel the benefit of higher profits.

Maintaining a relationship with suppliers

Once you've established a network of suppliers you're happy with and can rely on, it's important you maintain a good working relationship with them. It's not just about paying your bills on time.

- Try to deal with the same sales representative or agent whenever you order. Building a relationship with one person is more likely to inspire trust and the odd favour when you need it.
- Keep a check on prices and review your bills against what other suppliers are offering. Even if you don't want to change suppliers you may be able to negotiate more competitive prices. Don't be afraid to do this, suppliers will understand your need to get a good price and be grateful

for giving them the chance to match it rather than lose your trade to a competitor.

- Remember not to judge a supplier solely on price. Ensure levels of customer service, flexibility and, crucially, quality of product don't slip.

IN MY EXPERIENCE:

Paul Mather, Sherston Post Office Stores

You have to respect your size and lack of purchasing power initially and accept that some offers won't be the best in the world. You use experience to negotiate as time progresses, but if suppliers are being unreasonable, walk away.

Building good credit

In an ideal world we'd all be paid the minute we invoice and be given as long as we want to pay – and some companies, often the big ones with lots of weight to throw around, take that attitude. It won't even be an option for you as a start-up as suppliers will look to be paid promptly, but view this as a positive opportunity to build trust and earn the right to greater flexibility going forward.

If you do buy on credit, make keeping payments up-to-date a real priority. Falling behind with repayments is the best way to ruin an otherwise good business relationship and if a supplier suddenly withholds delivery or demands payment of what you owe in full, your business's future could be in real jeopardy.

Things to remember:

● Have a clear idea of what you are looking for: especially price and quality.

● Try to buy in bulk, or ask for discounts.

● Build up a mutually beneficial relationship with your supplier.

● When researching importing, don't forget to add up the cost of transport and customs tax.

Recruiting staff

I t's no coincidence that when entrepreneurs collect awards the one thing almost all of them attribute their success to is their employees. The fact that they recognise the need to do this possibly also tells you why they're up there grabbing the gongs, too. The people you employ to help run your shop will have just as much influence over its success as the goods that you sell, so it's crucial you get the right team on board. Recruitment is a tricky area, and one that ends up extremely costly if you make bad decisions.

Like your business plan you have to plan carefully and decide what roles you need filled, be that an experienced sales person or a shelf stacker you will need to train up, as well as the number of staff your shop will need to be a success. This chapter will guide you from defining the kind of team you need, through the recruitment process, to the paperwork you will need to file once you hire someone. It also contains advice on training your staff to ensure your shop reaches its full potential, and how to cope with the mantra 'the customer is always right'.

In this chapter we'll look at:

- Identifying your staffing needs
- Writing job descriptions
- Writing a job advert
- Interviewing

- Training up your new recruits
- Ways of attracting the best talent
- Pitfalls to watch out for
- The necessary paperwork

➡ WHAT ARE YOUR STAFFING NEEDS?

Your business plan should have included an idea of how many members of staff you'll need to run your shop smoothly, but also will have taken into account what you can afford. Ask yourself the following questions:

- How many members of staff does the shop require at any one time?
- Will you need more staff on certain days than others?
- Will you need more staff at certain times of the year?
- What will be your busiest or most staff intensive hours?
- Do you require a shop manager who will be more senior than sales assistants?
- How much can you increase sales by adding an extra member of staff?

FROM THE EXPERTS:
John Spooner, Monsoon

As a rule of thumb, staff shouldn't cost more than 10% of revenue.

Once you've established exactly how many members of staff your shop needs you will have to make a decision on what you can afford to pay them. You'll need to strike a fine balance between being practical and not stretching your budget too far, but also being realistic about what you need to pay to attract the right kind of talent.

FROM THE EXPERTS:
Mike Clare, Dreams plc

Motivate people with monetary incentives; you should always have incentives and bonuses. People might want flexitime, job satisfaction and career development, but at the end of the day they're working for money.

Retail is notoriously low paid and has high levels of turnover. This makes staff affordable and arguable easy to find but also hard to keep hold of. To gain

loyalty you'll have to think of ways
to keep staff and at this level it's
likely most people will be working to
either progress their careers or to earn
money to fund something they enjoy
better.

> ### TIP
>
> Most shops incentivise staff
> with bonuses or commission on sales
> and this can work well.

Distinguishing job roles

Store manager

For many people, the whole point of opening a shop is running it on a day-
to-day basis. It might be a social desire to mix with the public or work with
family; it might be a professional motivation to have control of ordering and
displaying stock, managing the floor etc. Whatever the reason, they want to be
in control, involved, the epicentre of all activity. And there's absolutely nothing
wrong with that. Many great shops thrive on the passion and personality of their
owners.

For others though, often those shop owners looking to expand quickly or
with outside interests who don't intend to be onsite full-time, there's a need for
someone else to fill the manager's role.

It's a tricky appointment and in less litigious days it wasn't uncommon for shop
owners to burn through a few managers before they found one they liked. You'll
need to be more careful about selecting the right person in the first place. After
all the hard work you put into starting the business, this person will have a major
say in its success.

As we tackle later in this section, the key starting point for any successful
recruitment is a clear job description. However, aside from experience and skills,
you'll need to find someone who you get on with, can trust and someone who
shares your vision for the business.

You'll need your store manager to be motivated to drive sales and the obvious
way to do that is through commission and bonuses. Better than a straight
percentage are staggered bonuses or commission incentives above certain target
thresholds incentivising them to keep striving for the next level. You'll also find
loyalty in making them feel valued through training and further management
opportunities should the company grow.

Sales assistants

While not sharing the same level of responsibility as a store manager, sales assistants will play a big role in your shop's performance. They could be responsible for the first impression, shopping experience and lasting memory from your shop. And as we all know from our various experiences as customers, the level of courtesy, knowledge and helpfulness displayed by staff is a massive factor in how we view a shop, how we communicate that experience to other people and, consequently, whether we return shop or others visit on our word of mouth recommendation.

When you consider that entry level sales assistants in the retail trade are one of the lowest paid professions with one of the highest levels of churn, the challenge of finding staff that are passionate, knowledgeable and motivated ambassadors of your brand is somewhat intensified.

The secret is this: you don't find them, you make them. You invest time into explaining what you expect of them, you train them and give them the knowledge you'd like them to impart and you pay and incentivise them to perform to these standards and stay loyal. You show them they're important to you and that you're willing to share your profits with them, no matter how modestly, because they're part of your vision and you've shared aims.

IN MY EXPERIENCE:

Lance Prebble, Pole Position

The skill in being a sales assistant is in the psychology of judging who wants to be left alone and who wants to be helped without being too obtrusive or unobtrusive.

That said, if we're honest, a significant majority of people working in retail don't have any aspirations of forging a career in retail or even care that much how well the business is doing providing it pays their wages and isn't too unpleasant or intensive. For many it's a means to an end and no matter how passionate you are, you'll need to appreciate that and work with it. After all, most of us have been there at some time or another.

TIP
Look at what types of incentives and perks you can offer staff from store discounts, commission, drinks down the pub, flexi-time, fun days out or sponsoring sports and charity activities. Keep it varied to keep it fresh and try and set new targets for individuals and teams to be aiming towards.

Most importantly, lead by example. If you're not punctual, smartly turned out, positive, polite and motivated, then you've no right to expect your staff to be. If you're having a bad day, you've argued with your partner, the bailiffs are ringing non-stop and your suppliers are threatening to withhold your order it's your job to put a smile on your face and convince the team it's business as usual so they convey that to customers.

IN MY EXPERIENCE:

Clare Thommen, Boudiche

We made some early mistakes. We recruited a lovely girl who had bra fitting experience with a large department store as we knew fitting was important to us. However you can train someone to fit a bra, you can't train attitude and I remember hearing in horror one day as she asked a VIP customer taking an item into the fitting room, 'do you know how much that costs?'.

Casual staff

Lots of shops rely on casual staff, especially for peaks and troughs in trade such as weekends and holiday seasons. It's also a sensible way to start recruiting if you're not entirely sure you need anyone full-time.

An ideal situation to try and establish is a flexible team of reliable casual staff who you can call upon when needed and whom you could possibly employ full-time if the opportunity arises. Students can make great casual staff as well, both during term times and those returning home for the holidays. Try to keep a pool of both and keep an eye out for replacements when they graduate. If they happen to be your target audience, students can also be great advocates to have on your side – provided you treat them well, of course!

Be prepared to give the same flexibility you expect in return: it's perfectly reasonable that someone can't work for you at short notice if they're not on your

payroll. It's best to be clear about when you expect them to work, especially over key dates such as bank holidays and Christmas.

➡ RECRUITING STAFF

The key to successful recruiting is to put the homework in up front. It's tempting to rush out and get a job ad out and applications in, but for several reasons, that isn't the way to go about it.

Start by drawing up a detailed job description of the duties and responsibilities of the role and the attributes, skills and experience needed from candidates. The more closely you define the role, the more likely you will be to get applicants that meet your requirements.

Recruitment has become embroiled in employment law in recent years with a number of high profile cases where business owners have been taken to tribunals on grounds of discrimination for not employing someone because of their race, gender, disability, sexuality or religious belief.

Being morally resolute that such a repugnant thought would never cross your mind sadly isn't enough to keep you covered from claims of discrimination. It's quite possible someone might see a fault in your recruitment process and look to take advantage or you might inadvertently cause upset by your reason for rejecting a candidate.

A prime example was a case from early 2008 where a hair salon owner was taken to a tribunal for unfair discrimination on grounds of religious belief because she refused a Muslim girl she'd interviewed and met only once for 15 minutes for a job on the basis that she felt staff should sport haircuts that reflected the urban attitude of the salon and the girl had stated she wouldn't remove her headscarf if she got the position.

The tribunal actually decided the salon owner's explanation was reasonable and rejected the claim for discrimination but did order her to pay £4,000 for 'hurt feelings'. According the vagaries of the law she could actually have been found guilty in the first place because she hadn't specified the requirement to sport the salon's haircuts in the job ad and so effectively had treated the girl differently.

Writing job descriptions

Therein lies the crux. Your job description (and advertisement) should lay out the criteria by which you shall recruit. If you have specific requirements which you can legally justify (ie It's not ok to say you'll only employ men for a general position, but it is if that role is to assist in a men's fitting room), then providing you detail them in advance and expose every candidate to the same criteria you cannot be accused of discriminating against one candidate. That's why it's essential to spend time planning at the beginning of the recruitment process.

Once you've established a firm criteria and requirements for the role, prioritise them into primary and secondary requirements. This will give you a firm matrix to compare applications and interviews so that if any legal objection was ever raised you'd have clear written evidence that the process was fair and above board.

This might seem an onerous process for recruiting what might be a shop assistant but as well as protecting you legally, it should also set you in good stead for finding the right person to make life easier. And once you've done it once, you can use the same process again.

Advertising for staff

Once you've made a detailed job description, making out an ad should be easy. List all the job requirements, criteria for applicants, information about your shop and also state the salary or wage you'll pay. Some people advise against this but by listing what you're prepared to pay you're ensuring you don't waste your time vetting applications from candidates expecting to earn more than you can afford to pay.

Just as important as what you detail about the job role, is the information on how you want people to reply. Be specific. Ideally you want everyone to reply in the same way so you're making a fair and direct comparison of applications. The best way to do this is to use application forms but you might not have the time to draw one up or deem them not personal enough. If you want CVs then ask for a personal letter as well. Try and tailor the response to the skills of the role. Courtesy and people skills is likely to be important so perhaps ask applicants to explain why they have those attributes in their letters. If you need someone to take orders over the phone it might be that you ask people to apply that way. If IT skills are important then applications by email only is another way of vetting.

Where you advertise will depend on the role and type of shop you're running. For more senior positions such as store manager it might be that you target people already working in retail through the retail press or recruitment websites or agencies that can prove they've strong retail candidates on their books. Targeted advertising can make more sense than more general options, but be careful about what you're spending. It could be that online message boards such as gumtree, notice boards, networking contacts, job centres or even the good old fashioned ad in the window could be just as effective. Most likely, a combination will produce a decent response.

Short-listing candidates for interview

You'll already have done the hard work and this is where your matrix should pay dividends. Simply pass all your applications past your primary and secondary criteria ticking each attribute that they meet. If you've three candidates that meet all the primary boxes they're clearly the best suited for the job. If you have none then start consulting the secondary options and so on.

Be careful that you use this criteria and this criteria only. After all, you made it. Bringing any other consideration into an isolated application could be discriminatory if you don't then apply the same to all the others.

It's likely confusion will occur when an application meets most of the criteria but either lets itself down in someway such as poor spelling or incorrect information supplied, or you have a gut feeling the person could give you more in an interview than on paper. It's unrealistic to pretend gut feeling doesn't exist and actually it's damned important because after all you're going to have to work closely with this person so it can't be a purely mathematical choice. Providing you're not discriminating against someone on gut feeling you should be fine and, remember, the interview process is just as important as the overall application.

Look to make a manageable shortlist but remember it's very risky to reject someone for an interview if they've met the same criteria as everyone else unless you've got a very good reason you'd be prepared to stand in front of a tribunal to defend.

Interviewing

Successful interviewing requires certain skills. If you've never employed people before you may find some training helpful. For more information on training contact the Chartered Institute of Personnel and Development at www.cipd. co.uk. There are various courses available to teach you effective interviewing techniques, but if you can't spare the time or finances for these, we'll cover the basics here.

Interviews must be planned extremely carefully. You only have a short window of time to elicit all the information you need for a potential recruit. Not only do you have to ascertain their relevant levels of experience, you also need to gauge accurate impressions about whether they fit in with the kind of atmosphere you're trying to achieve.

After coming up with a shortlist for interview, you should contact prospective interviewees and give them clear instructions on where you're located, how to get there, what they should bring with them, who they should ask for and how long the process is likely to last.

> **TIP**
>
> If you've already found your shop then it's a good idea to conduct the interview there so people get an immediate feel for what the place and the business.

Set aside some dedicated time to do the interviews – make sure there's no unnecessary interruptions such as ringing phones or other staff or even family members vying for your attention. To ensure you're not interrupted put a sign on the door along the lines of 'Interview taking place – do not disturb'. It might sound ridiculously basic, but it's amazing what a difference this simple measure makes.

Remember, the interview stage is just as much about selling yourself and the shop to them as the other way around. The best candidates are always going to be in high demand so you'll need to impress them too if you want to attract them to work for you. Think ahead about how to begin the interview by explaining a little bit about yourself, how you've got to stage you're at, what your plans are for the business and what you're looking for in a candidate.

Preparing to interview candidates

It's also good practice to explain how you see the interview going, even it's to say it's going to be an informal chat for 15 mins. This should put the candidate at ease, help them relax and enable you to see their more natural personality. You learn far less from someone if they're nervous, uptight and adopting a false front. One of the main advantages of taking the time to refresh yourself on an interviewee's application before they arrive is that you can ask them a few light questions about their interests to help them relax.

Prepare your questions in advance by returning to your initial job specification. Include general questions regarding their personality, as well as questions that probe more deeply into how well suited they are to the job, but, again, make sure you ask all candidates the same questions that are likely to be decisive in your decision making and don't tackle issues of a sensitive issue that aren't relevant to the job. Ask open questions that encourage fuller responses.

Include any written or practical test you think might be relevant but it's usually fair to tell candidates about this beforehand. Give interviewees the opportunity to ask you questions, but don't feel you need to answer anything you aren't comfortable answering and never immediately reveal how an interviewee has got on.

If you think it's appropriate get the serious candidates in for second interview and if you have someone else in the business at this stage, consider involving them for a second opinion.

TIP

Some of the largest stores actually involve shop floor staff in the interview process for management to test interviewees' people skills with different groups. Another trick is to ask other members of staff to show interviewees in and out of the premises and to the interview room as you'll find people tend to be far more relaxed in this situation and ask very different questions to other staff than they'll ask to you, the boss.

Throughout the process keep clear notes that relate directly back to the primary and secondary requirements you first set out. It could be that you make out a tick box form in advance or mark a score next to each point, which is far easier than trying to scribble full notes and less intimidating.

The selection process

Once you've completed the interview process, if you've done as outlined, you should have one clear candidate and it's likely because you've been so clear in your thinking throughout that your gut feeling will be closely aligned to what's on paper. If there's not one clear choice then it's time to study your feedback and make a decision. Once you've done that and you're happy you've got the right person then contact them by phone, set a start date and confirm in writing.

➡ THE PAPERWORK

Becoming an employer for the first time can seem a little daunting. There's a whole raft of administrative duties you'll now be responsible for, and neglecting them is not an option.

Your first point of call should be to contact HMRC on 0845 60 70 143 and request a New Employer Starter Pack. It contains everything you need to set yourself up to recruit staff.

Nearly everyone that will work in your shop will count as an employee, which means you need to be aware of your obligations for tax and National Insurance contributions. You must keep detailed records of every single member of staff right from the very beginning. All of the following types of staff count as employees in the eyes of the taxman:

- Directors
- Full and part-time workers
- Temporary or casual workers

Even if a worker claims to be self-employed and will pay their own tax and National Insurance, as an employer it is your responsibility to confirm that. HMRC will offer you guidance on how to do this in the Starter Pack.

Of course, making sure your employees' tax is in order isn't the only obligation you have. Make sure you also know your legal responsibilities regarding:

- Statutory sick and maternity pay
- Working time and pay regulations
- National Minimum Wage
- Redundancy pay
- Employing foreign nationals
- Part-time workers' regulations

➡ INDUCTION AND TRAINING

Think ahead to your new person's first day. There's nothing worse than starting a new job and it being clear nobody's really ready for you. You're a start-up so it won't do your new person any harm to learn quickly that they'll have to take situations as they come, but it's important to set out clear expectations from minute one.

On their first day, sit them down, detail what you expect from them, how you'll assess their performance, how they will be rewarded, who they will report to and all the other information you'll need to cover such as holidays, pay, where the toilets and fire exits are etc. Just as importantly, explain to them your vision for the company, what the USPs and identity of the shop is and how you expect customers to be treated. It's your baby but the more people you can get sharing the vision the more chance you've got of seeing it blossom.

Be careful that you train people for any jobs they need to do or tasks that are likely to invoke health and safety legislation (see legal issues, p??) and make frequent and regular assessments to identify training needs. The more you make your people feel cared for and invested in, the more loyal they will be.

Things to remember:

- Limit recruiting staff until you've seen not just predicted what demand is. Recruit as you need people.

- Work out exactly what you require in each role before you start recruiting for the job and come up with a clear job description.

- Put an ad in your window for casual staff.

- Be careful not to fall into any interview traps regarding questions about personal or family life. It could land you in hot water and contravene employment law.

The opening

U nbolting those doors and flicking the closed sign to open is the day you've waited for and worked so hard to get to. From raw idea to writing a business plan, securing premises, kitting them out and buying in stock, you're finally ready to start trading and, hopefully, make some money. Before you can do that however, you need to get the customers through the doors.

In this chapter we'll take you through the process of launching your shop with the right level of publicity to get interested customers through your door and satisfied buyers back out.

You will need to decide what kind of advertising will work best for you, be that press releases, print ads or online advertising, and whether you want to hire a professional PR firm to organise this for you.

In this chapter we'll cover:

- PR
- Advertising
- First impressions
- Soft openings
- Launch parties

 # PR AND ADVERTISING

If you're reading this heading thinking, 'but I haven't got much (if any) money left for advertising', you're actually very sensible. Throwing money at advertising a new shop isn't always the most sensible approach, especially until you've, shall we say, ironed out the creases that'll inevitably crop up in the first few months of trading.

When you're first starting out there's a lot of PR (public relations) and self-promotion you can do for relatively little budget. If you're adamant you need to start paying for ads from day one, you'll need a clear strategy to ensure you're getting maximum return on your investment and are able to measure the effect your spend has had.

PR

PR is coverage of your business in magazine, newspapers, websites or TV, radio or even podcasts and webinars. For publications with any credibility, it is promotion you can't buy and so is hugely influential. Compared to advertising where you're simply paying to appear on a page, billboard, web banner etc, it's assumed your business is being written about because someone thinks it's worthy of coverage. Providing the reason for that is positive and that the reader respects the publication, that's a very powerful endorsement.

As a journalist and former editor of Startups.co.uk, I've received thousands of press releases from new companies looking for PR coverage. Many of them led to us writing profiles, news stories and features offering months of free publicity in front of an audience of more than 100,000 people every month for shops that had literally just opened their doors. Admittedly, others went straight in the bin. Believe me, that's the same in every newsroom from The Times to Model Railway Monthly.

The difference between those covered and binned though rarely has much to do with the actual business. Sure, if you're opening the world's first money tree shop you'd probably make a frontpage splash no matter how screwed up the press release, but most of the time, for all you ordinary businesses, it's about pointing out the one thing which makes you not so ordinary – and if you've followed our planning section you'll have plenty of USPs to plug.

Press releases

Pitching to journalists shouldn't be too different to pitching to the bank. You're looking to inspire them and tell them what they need to know to do business with you. They need to hear what's so great about your story and there's a story in every business somewhere, it's just a case of digging it out.

The key is finding the angle. It's not news that you're simply opening a cake shop. There's millions of those. It is news if your cakes are 50% better for you than any other shop's. Equally, it is news if yours are most calorific this side of chocolate heaven. It is news if Gordon Ramsay says he likes them. It is news if you trained under the most famous pastry chef in the land. It is news if you used to be a fitness trainer and you've swapped it for a life of cakemaking.

If you're blankly thinking, 'but I don't have anything interesting like that', then the answer is to engineer an angle. It is news if you're going to give away a cake to every customer on your first day of opening, it is news if you're going to hold a cake eating competition, if you've changed your name to Mr. Cake Man. It is news if you're making a special coloured cake to match the strip of the local football team.

Think niches as well; if you're using eco packaging that's interesting to an eco title; if you're offering diet products target magazines and newspaper columns for slimmers; if you're the first cake shop to open in your area for 20 years point that out to the local papers. Every business has a PR story it's just a case of sculpting it and pointing it out to the right people.

You should always start by doing this yourself. Try and get as many of these little unique stories saved in your head as possible because you'll find them invaluable when talking to a whole range of people, not just journalists, about why your business is so great. For actually getting coverage, you've two choices. Go direct yourself or use a PR company.

Using a PR company

If you've got budget, PR companies can be massively useful. The two key elements you'll be paying for are their wealth of contacts and their management of the whole process. Any PR company worth its salt will keep up-to-date on who occupies all the key editorial positions in all media organisations, has strong working relationships with them and can get a story to the right person. They should also look to apply their expertise to manage a full publicity campaign, staggering stories in different publications to achieve maximum exposure over a period of time. With all the other elements of running a shop to take care of, it's highly unlikely you'll have time to do this yourself and will end up snatching at publicity from any title that bites.

IN MY EXPERIENCE:

Clare Thommen, Boudiche

My advice: PR, PR and more PR!

While I've seen plenty that can't, PR companies should also be able to write a good press release – but for sanity's sake, you should ask to check everything before it goes out.

If you can't afford a PR company from day one, which I'm imagining will be the case for most of you, have a go at doing it yourself. Target the titles you think should be most interested in your story, call them up to ask who the best person to send press releases to is, then put one together and send it off. Here are some useful tips for writing a press release.

- Make sure the wording is correct, the message is clear and direct and the correct information is provided so that a journalist will be able to use it even if they do not contact a member of your company or PR team.
- Your release should convey a sense of importance but not seem over-hyped. You want to provide information about your firm in a newsy format, not a marketing letter. Besides, if your announcement is worth sending a release out about, it can probably stand on its own without marketing hype.
- All press releases should answer the journalist's five basic questions of: Who, What, Where, Why and How. This will require you to put yourself in the shoes of a journalist and chances are, answering those questions will give you a clearer idea of what you want to write.
- A punchy headline should be included that matches the release's first sentence, or lead, as those in the trade call them. The headline should be factual. It shouldn't try to make a joke or be smart.
- The first sentence should be direct, relate what is going on, convey a level of importance of the news and start off with the name of your shop.
- Include a quote from you about why you've decided to open the shop. Quotes personalise stories and give journalists an idea of who to speak to. Most journalists will seek their own quotes by following up releases with interviews, but having a quote gives journalists the option to use it.
- Contact details for journalists who want to find out more can either go at the top of the release or the bottom.

One thing to remember is journalists get inundated with hundreds of releases and sometimes even the best ones get overlooked, so don't get upset if you don't get a response. If you haven't heard anything within a couple of days, call the person you sent it to and ask them if they thought it was relevant. If it wasn't, ask them why so you can tailor it closer to their needs next time.

TIP

If a publication calls you and say they'll feature you for a cost, don't do it. Paid for articles have zero credibility and regardless of what the person on the end of the phone tells you, aren't read. Politely refuse.

➡ ADVERTISING

Print ads

The most common forms of print advertising that small businesses use are:

- Local/regional/national newspapers
- Trade journals
- Trade directories
- Telephone directories eg Yellow Pages
- Miscellaneous items such as calendars, local tourist information

Newspapers and magazines should provide an audited readership profile, which can be matched to the customer profile to identify if they'll attract the right kind of customers to your shop. They should be able to provide you with information on their circulation, which is the amount of copies that go out. Avoid advertising in publications without this kind of audited data.

TIP

While it's important to do your research on the circulation of whoever you advertise with, bear in mind that free newspapers and magazines may have a readership lower than the official circulation. In contrast, those with a cover price usually have a readership larger than circulation.

In terms of size, generally, the bigger the better if budget permits, although putting editorial onto the page either at the bottom or the left-hand side can actually help. You should also bear in mind that as print ads are repeated the impact lessens. It can, therefore, be better to spend the budget on a few high impact ads than a lot of small ones. But test the waters slowly. Don't blow your whole marketing budget on a massive ad campaign in the local newspaper only to find print ads aren't the right medium for you.

Publishers will quote you different rates for different positions and sizes. Prime spots such as near the front or in the news sections, right hand pages, or tops of pages cost about 20% more but as a rule are worth the extra investment because they're viewed by the most readers. If you're going to splash out on an advert to let people know you're open for business you could use the opportunity to run a special offer.

Sample prices

- Quarter page ad in a local paper can cost upwards of £250 depending on its circulation
- A full page ad in a national paper such as *The Daily Mail* can cost in the region of £30,000

Always negotiate. The first price is never the best price. Find out when the last possible deadline is before the publication goes to press then phone back. While you might not get your preferred slot, most sales people will give you heavy discounts on unsold slots just to get them filled.

FROM THE EXPERTS:
John Spooner, Monsoon

National ads are far too extravagant. For local press, it's better to know the editor and see if he'll do an editorial – although you might have to pay for this as well.

Online advertising

Online advertising overtook print in terms of total spend some time ago and is closing in fast on TV. That's pretty much the reason why even if you've got zero desire to spend online you should look at getting a simple website made to advertise who you are, what you do and how people can find you.

Over 90% of web traffic comes from search and for search, read Google. While you should look to optimise your website to appear in the central, natural Google search, the easiest way to advertise your website online is using pay-per-click advertising which Google calls AdWords. These are the small advertisements you see down the right side of Google.

It's very simple. You set up a campaign by identifying the search terms you'd like to appear against (cake shop, Leeds for example), put a limit on how much you want to spend and you only pay when someone actually clicks on your ad and goes through to your website.

In terms of measuring return on investment you won't get a more accurate media for advertising, providing you factor in the cost of getting a simple website built and hosted of course.

Radio/TV advertising

As the web has ploughed ahead, the development of digital radio and TV has meant prices to advertise have tumbled, while the choice of audiences has widened. TV will possibly be outside your price range as a start-up shop, but if you'd like to explore this option then contact a small local production company experienced at producing broadcast advertisements on limited budgets.

You'll need to take a similar approach for radio, which can be effective at a local level. For radio particularly, it's worth speaking to the sales teams of stations to ask the optimum length and style of ads and any recommendations for production firms to work with.

Yellow Pages/directories

The days where if you were running a shop then you simply had to be in Yellow Pages are long gone. That said, it can still be very effective if your shop provides a relatively unusual service people naturally need to search for or if your shop is tucked away. Directories work best for companies where people aren't automatically aware of their location or don't use frequently, such as plumbers, builders or maybe even food takeaways.

If you think you'd pick up business from Yellow Pages, negotiate a trial period to see what success you have. If they don't agree to this, negotiate until they do as they'll almost always prefer to give you this than put the phone down without 'a sale'.

➡ SOFT OPENINGS AND LAUNCH PARTIES

A lot of shops get it spectacularly wrong during their first few weeks so be wary about shouting your arrival from the roughtops too fervently. While you certainly want people to know you're open, trading and more than happy to take their money, it might make sense to leave it a couple of weeks before you 'officially launch'.

Launch doesn't have to equal 'day one'. Far better to get open, spot all the little problems and have time to put them right than fill your shop full of expectant key influencers and watch them pick out all the imperfections you could have sorted out with a little more time.

Soft launch

Soft launches, as they're called, make far more sense. Get the doors open and start trading, speak to customers about how they find the shop and what they'd like to see. Use the first few weeks to make sure staff are trained properly and are providing the right level of customer service.

Try and offer a few incentives during these first few weeks to get customers in and garner their feedback. Offer introductory discounts (be careful not to make this look too much like a desperate sale), free opening purchase gifts or even run a competition where you can collect customers contact details in order to invite them to an official opening.

> ## ⚡ TIP
> Keep the first few weeks nice and relaxed (even if you're feeling the opposite inside) and keep your eyes and ears open for any way you can improve the service you're offering.

Launch party

Just because you've 'soft launched' it doesn't mean you shouldn't later have an official launch party. In fact, you absolutely must! Here's your first chance to pull in a crowd and stand out from all the other shops in the row or centre.

If you've hired a PR company, they should ensure local journalists are present, lured by the prospect of a great story and a glass of bubbly (wine if budgets are really tight) and hopefully a local celebrity or council member. If you're doing it yourself, make a list of targets, send out some invitations (email is sufficient) and follow-up with confirmation calls and a reminder email on the day.

Just as importantly, work hard to get your target customers in. Look at complimentary associations or clubs where you can advertise your launch, while even a poster in the window and giving out leaflets on the street can work well.

You'll need an incentive for shoppers so advertise a 'one night only' discount for those attending the launch. Print up some vouchers and give them out on the door as people enter and then again as the leave, providing an incentive for them to return.

On the night, make the evening as entertaining as possible. This is your one chance to make a first impression, so go all out. You should be on a complete charm offensive whether it comes to you naturally or not, and try to speak to every person even if it's to simply introduce yourself and thank them for coming. Oh, and stay sober! Even if you're nervous, let the others do the drinking. Nobody likes a drunken host!

> **FROM THE EXPERTS:**
> ### John Spooner, Monsoon
>
> Launch razzmatazz is high risk for start-ups and while it can pay off if you get it right, a soft launch probably makes more sense.

Things to remember:

- Don't pay for advertising where free PR can be more effective.

- Negotiate hard on any ads you buy or directories you join.

- Soft launch first in order to tweak any imperfections.

- Pull in a crowd and go on a charm offensive for your big launch.

Electronic Article Surveillance: How do you know what your shop needs?

UK retail loses around £1.6 billion per year to theft. Theft, or shrinkage, is typically between 0.5-3% of the total sales of a shop, which obviously can be the difference between making profit or not in your first critical stages!

Whilst organised theft will always persist, it is possible to reduce its occurrence, and deter casual shoplifters. By investing in security systems you can help staff remotely and covertly protect your shop's merchandise – and ultimately your profits. The two most commonly used technologies are CCTV and Electronic Article Surveillance (EAS).

CCTV is used to monitor high risk areas of your shop, for example low visibility aisles or areas which merchandise high value, highly desirable goods. EAS involves the application of various tags and adhesive labels that will alarm security gates at the shop exit if product is illicitly removed. When merchandise is purchased correctly, the tags and labels are removed at the Point of Sale.

When selecting an EAS system
- Firstly consider the brand and aesthetics of your shop. You can make the gates look as visible or as invisible as you like, but you may be restricted by the type of doorway in your shop.
- Secondly, ensure that all costs are taken into consideration. You will need to calculate the full cost of installation, hardware, tags and labels, and any service plan offered.
- Finally, to maximise the effectiveness of an EAS system, all components should be tested on a daily basis to check they are working correctly.

Once you have the basic platform, there is a plethora of security tags to chose from that beep and flash to ensure that thieves know that your store is not an easy target! Correct, well managed deployment of EAS will enable you to show off your best products, as customers are most likely to only buy what they see is available and well displayed.

But remember, do not become over zealous with your approach to tagging. You are trying to prevent theft, not sales.

If you would like unbiased advice about tagging and which technology would suit you, call TAG Company on **0800 781 3598** or visit their website **www.tagcompany.com**

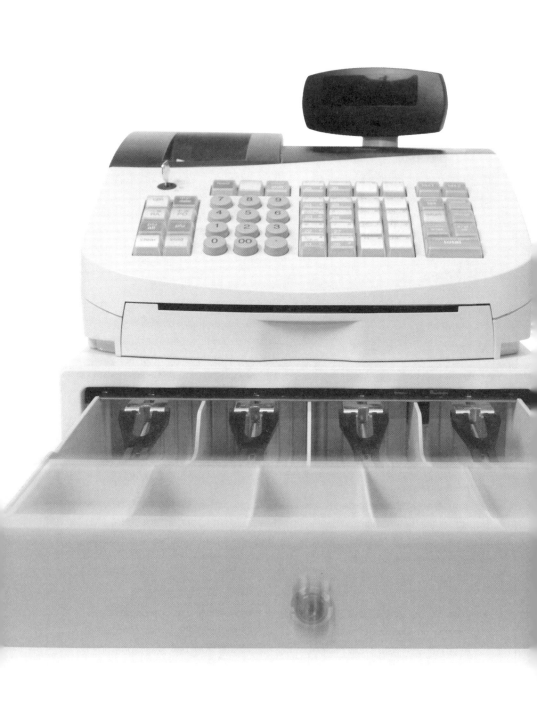

3

You're open

3.1

Surviving the first six months

The doors are open. The launch party is over. Your staff are trained and you're even on first-name terms with Bob from the cash 'n' carry. You're the master of your own destiny sitting pretty in your own shop, picking the hours you want to work. This is the point where anyone who's already progressed beyond this point breaks into a knowing chuckle because, as you'll soon find out, getting open is only half the battle. Staying open is the real challenge.

You need to be prepared for an inevitably slow beginning. But this can be a great opportunity to hone your operation and make sure everything is running perfectly. It can also be a good time to reassess your USPs, and try out different opening times to see what works best for you. This is the time when you learn to deal with complaints and get some experience of working with your suppliers. The first few months are a matter of survival.

In this chapter we'll cover:
- Preparing for a slow start
- Adapting your idea and systems
- Pricing
- Contingency budgets
- New trends
- Opening hours

➡ PREPARING FOR A SLOW START

Don't panic. You should prepare for your first few weeks to be fairly slow so don't freak out when they are. It's always going to take a while for word to get out and for passing trade to venture in. In turn, don't bury your head in the sand either and use the time wisely. A slow start is not necessarily a bad thing, as it can give you a chance to hone your operation. A slower start allows you to perfect your model, test your ideas and assess what works.

> **IN MY EXPERIENCE:**
> ## Clare Thommen, Boudiche
>
> It was terrible! Scary!! We cried lots. We had no idea how hard it would be. The retail model is just so cash unfriendly. You have buy all your stock by ordering in advance so you've continually got cash tied up in stock. Our sales weren't anywhere near what we'd forecast.

As your reputation in the area builds, so too should your customer base. You should have accounted for a gradual increase in trade in your business plan anyway. The key to surviving the first few months is doing everything you can to keep the cash flowing in, while keeping overheads low. Too many shops actually get more than enough customers through the door and purchases through the door, but suffer because their overheads are disproportionately high.

From the first month's trading, adjust your stock levels so you're not carrying more than you need to. Don't cut back your product range, just buy what you can best predict you're likely to sell and keep as much cash as you can in the pot. Similarly don't go employing staff until you absolutely need them and if you do, take people on a casual basis first explaining a permanent role will follow as soon as you can afford it.

Taking advantage of free time

While trade is slower this may a good opportunity to bring in some of your marketing skills. Think about the different kinds of special offers you can introduce to try and boost trade. Avoid emblazoning your shop with the word 'sale' as this can portray desperation more than invitation, but don't be scared to use calls to action in the window such as 'introduction offer', 'just opened', 'come in and see our great selection of . . . '.

The Ongoing Marketing chapter gives you far more detail on this but it's something to consider during your early stages of trading. You should also look to stagger PR throughout the first six months. If you've come up with five great PR stories, don't use them all for the launch and keep in regular contact with journalists. If you've had a great month, press release it, if you've had a celebrity visitor advertise it; keep thinking how you can make the news and stay fresh in people's minds.

If you've any budget for marketing, overcoming the lull that inevitably follows the highs of a launch month is the time to spend it. It's actually much better to spend money on advertising after a month or so because by then people might have seen your shop, know where you are and be more influenced to pop in – that's a far more likely scenario than reacting to advert for a shop you've never heard of before.

More than anything, stay calm but focussed. Measure everything. Record everything. You should know the unit sales of every product, what you're making most mark-up on and not just how many sales each member of staff is making, but how cost-effective they

> ### ⭐ TIP
> The first six months should teach you about your business and your customers – like any other relationship, you'll need to get to know one another and if you don't work at it, nothing will improve.

are for you. Resist outlandish, wholesale changes and stick to your identity and business plan, but carry out subtle experiments with lay-out, and perhaps even products and opening hours and measure the impact.

➡ ADAPTING YOUR IDEA

While your first six months should be a constant learning process, there is a point where you need to stop, take stock and ask if the business is ever going to work without some wholesale changes.

If you've been tweaking, experimenting and measuring the impact of different approaches you'll be in a far better position to make the decision than if you've sat on your hands behind the counter hoping that miraculously you'll soon be swamped. Just because when you've pumped your life savings into a business, given up the safety of a salary and spent months developing your shop, it can then be massively difficult to accept it's not quite going as well you'd hoped.

Unfortunately, though, there are no assurances in business no matter how much planning and preparation you put in and the biggest celebrity entrepreneurs who sit on TV telling others how to do it have all had their flops – and will again.

The most important thing is to be open minded and prepare yourself in advance so if you do have to make some pretty drastic changes it won't come as a big shock – and if you don't want to lose face you can tell everyone that it was part of the plan all along!

Assessing what works

The key is to look at the business basics and get to the bottom of the problem. Go back to your business plan and hold it up to your shop. Is the shop you're sitting in a true reflection of the plan? If it is, then you need to look for what's going wrong. Usually it'll either be that you're not getting people through the door, that they're not buying, or, if they are, that you're pricing or supply line is wrong.

If when you compare your shop to the one in your business plan and you see something different then you could have found your answer. Is it true to the USPs and identity you outlined? Did you get lost or sidetracked on the original vision somewhere? Are you differentiating yourself enough and communicating the right messages as you'd originally intended? If you're not, then start reversing those problems and get back on track.

If you still can't work out where the problem lies, look at your finances because that's certainly where the problem will be hidden. Remember, it doesn't matter how many customers you have or how much you love your shop if it's losing money.

Money doesn't have to be your motivation for running a shop, but profit is your oxygen and you need to be striving for it in every buying and selling transaction.

> **FROM THE EXPERTS:**
> ## Mike Clare, Dreams plc
>
> Panic isn't a bad strategy! It gets the adrenaline and creative juices flowing. You need to do something different, don't just sit there – do something! Work harder!

Look at your suppliers. Can you source cheaper elsewhere? Can you buy better quality for the same price that would encourage more sales? Have you got any big overheads eating into your profit? If you have, be hard. Lose them. Yes, that includes people. Many, many entrepreneurs I've interviewed tell me their biggest regret is trying to grow their business too quickly, getting in a mess and having to lay people off to save it. However, many of them did it, survived as a consequence and went on to employee multiples of the people they upset by letting them go. If deliveries were a part of your business plan that can be shelved for a year; sell the van and pump the cash back into the rest of the shop.

> **TIP**
> Concentrate on the core business. If you're making big structural changes, update your business plan, then you've something to refer back to if you're still haemorrhaging money in a month's time.

New ideas / trends

One of the most common reasons any shop either fails to take off or sees trade drop is because it takes its eye off the ball. Retail moves like the wind so all that work you did researching the products your customers want and expect can never stop. Indeed, if you researched it and then spent three months fitting out the shop, it was probably out-of-date the minute you opened up.

It's more of a concern for some shops than others. If you're running a convenience store, change will be fairly slow and your core products won't change over 10 years. If you're in fashion or electrical market, anything longer than a three month cycle is archaic. You should always have a line of classic bestsellers but you need to stay in touch with the latest trends.

Buy the magazines your customers buy, know what and who they aspire to, visit the competition and work harder than them to find new suppliers and never miss a trade fair. You should be just as passionate and knowledgeable about the area or niche you're operating in as your customers are – in fact, you, your staff, your shop and even your website should be the experts in that area that the customers turn to for advice and guidance.

➡ CASHFLOW

Adjusting pricing

Take a look at your prices. Ensure you're not just selling at a price people can afford, but a price that's high enough to make your profit. Anyone can trick themselves into thinking they're doing a rich trade if they're pulling in the crowds by simply undercutting the competition. It's a perfectly acceptable strategy, of course, but only if you can do it and still make a profit. It's what the 'experts' mean when they say 'turnover is vanity, profit is sanity'.

If you're keen to offer discounted prices to incentivise customers, you need to claw that profit back elsewhere. Most retailers have some items, often referred to as 'loss leaders', that they use to pull in trade. Don't take this too literally, loss leaders should be sold at cost price, never at a loss. Look to do it with core items or where there's little margin to be made anyway.

On the flip side, if you're selling premium products that are one-off purchases, make sure you've a few cheaper items to get people through the door. Even the most luxurious high-end London department stores such as Harrods and Liberty ensure many of their ranges have something for everyone so window shoppers aren't discouraged from wandering in and target customers can justify a trip when they just happen to spend more than they anticipated.

✦ TIP

There's more on pricing in Managing the books (page 191).

Contingency budgets

No matter how well you manage your overheads against sales, the first six months of any business are by nature precarious and cashflow can be difficult to control. A contingency budget then is essential.

As a nation, we don't save anymore, as the credit crunch has proved. Culture is increasingly geared to living for the moment and the flexibility and choice that society offers lulls us, rightly or wrongly, into a belief that you can always find a solution to any situation. Don't take this ideology with you into business.

I can't articulate this enough: Businesses go bust for the stupidest of reasons and almost always it could have been avoided by a contingency budget. You're not setting money aside for a rainy day, you're doing it because you will need it. Even if your shop is ticking over nicely and generating a tidy profit, you need to expect the unexpected. If a supplier you've already paid for a shipment goes bust, where do you get your next stock from? If some idiot smashes your front window and you have to pay an emergency glazer £1,000 on the same day you're meant to pay for a delivery, then what?

There are too many shop skeletons haunting the high streets that could have gone on to be major chains worth hundreds of millions, but sunk because they were surviving perilously close to an overdraft limit when something unexpected occurred and the knock-on effects sent them under.

IN MY EXPERIENCE:
Clare Thommen, Boudiche

We had no cash buffer when the original bank funding was cut. We needed to buy stock for Christmas but hadn't sold what we'd got so we didn't have the cash. We ended up ordering it by credit card and paying 20% interest because otherwise we'd have gone under.

➡ OPENING HOURS

Be open. It doesn't get any simpler than that. It amazes me how so many new and small shops still only open 9–5, Monday to Saturday then complain that they can't compete with the big boys.

It's so much easier for a small independent shop to react to the increasing number of customers who prefer to shop outside these standard work hours, yet it's the big brands with huge workforces to co-ordinate that manage to do it. If enough buying customers to be profitable want you open at any hour then you should be open.

If you don't want to work those hours then fair enough. After all, you didn't escape the confines of working for someone else to become a slave to yourself. However, this is where you need to delegate and trust someone else to do it for you – and an unwillingness to do this is the reason many small shop owners are missing out on many more hours of lucrative trading.

Don't be afraid to delegate the responsibility of opening up and cashing up. If the biggest brands in the world can do it then so can you. If you trust people to work for you, then you should trust them to do this and the added responsibility will actually make them feel valued and promote loyalty. It'll also be to your advantage to have someone else who knows the ropes should, for any reason, you be taken away from the business at any point.

Things to remember:

- Don't expect a stampede of customers at first. Use a slower build up of trade as an opportunity to hone your operation.

- Don't bury your head in the sand and keep checking you're running the shop your customers want.

- Expect the unexpected and make sure you've a contingency budget.

- Be open!

Finance 2: Managing the books

Running a shop is what you set out to do and without doubt that's where your energies are best served. However, as you've had to do throughout this whole process, you'll always need to put time aside for the financial aspect of running a business. After all, that's what allows you to run the shop. You'll already have familiarised yourself with projections, forecasts and basic costings during the planning stage, but the reality of running any business is that you need a firm grip on the numbers at all times.

In this chapter we'll go through what type of records you need to keep, covering both the financial and management categories. We'll also outline the role of cashflow in your business and what type of VAT you will be required to pay. Now that your business is up and running you'll need to be aware of the daily financial issues of running that business, such as price changes, accepting payments and the all-important task of depositing your takings at the bank. You'll need to decide what accounting system you will use, and whether you'll be keeping records yourself or hiring the services of an accountant. You may not find it fun, but getting it right is essential.

In this chapter we'll cover:

- Accounts
- Balance sheets
- Profit and loss (P&L) sheets
- Cashflow forecasting

- VAT
- Day to day finances
- Managing payments
- Hiring an accountant
- Paying your staff

➡ ACCOUNTS

Running a business involves meticulous record-keeping, some of which you are obliged to do, and some of which simply helps you run your business more efficiently. Your accounts can be separated into two main categories – financial and management.

Financial

If your business is incorporated, ie a limited company, you are required by law to put together a set of financial records every year and file them with the Companies House. Unincorporated businesses are not required to do this; however they must still keep thorough accounting records to be used alongside their annual tax returns. You are obligated to keep a minimum of the last six years' worth of accounts for HMRC to call upon at any time.

There are detailed guidelines for how to prepare financial accounts on the Companies House website at www.companieshouse.gov.uk, but you will generally have to include the following:

- Balance sheet
- Profit and loss account
- Cashflow statement

Management

Your management accounts are the records you must keep in order to run your business well. This is where you'll cover everything, from how many units of stock are bought and sold, to the payroll data for your staff. You simply cannot run your shop efficiently without up-to-date and methodical records. You also need to take the necessary steps to ensure this information is stored safely and backed-up.

What records do you need to keep when running a shop? Well, your accounting records will be split into daily, weekly, monthly and annual figures, all of which are important. Efficient records will allow you to identify the strong and weak areas of your business and therefore take appropriate action in your day to day management and long-term planning.

> **FROM THE EXPERTS:**
> ## John Spooner, Monsoon
>
> Know your numbers within your abilities. No one expects you to be a chartered accountant and have all the clever answers, but a basic understanding of numbers is essential to understand the drivers of the business.

Records you should keep to have an accurate reflection of your shop's financial health include:

- All sales transactions broken down by date and product
- Stock levels – daily, weekly and monthly
- Receipts both for cash and credit card transactions
- Invoices from suppliers and service providers
- Any licences you require
- Property and lease documentation
- Staff shifts and wages
- Employee tax details
- Cost of other overheads including premises and utilities

It's important to note this is not a complete list, and you will need to add to it depending on the type of shop you run.

➡ BALANCE SHEETS

Essentially, reading a balance sheet is like checking your bank balance – it simply tells you what the business owes or owns at any particular time. But unlike your bank balance it doesn't just give you a number it also tells you what makes up that number. In essence the first part is everything your business owns – its assets. The second part is everything you owe – the liabilities.

The first part of the balance sheet should give you a figure that shows you the net worth of your business. That figure should also show in the second part of the business – also the net worth but working back from what capital you started with, any profits you have made and kept in the business or any money that you have taken out.

Here's a more detailed explanation of all of the sections of balance sheet.

- Fixed assets – this is typically anything that you count as an asset of the business but not something that you are likely to sell as part of your daily business. So include any premises, vans or other vehicles, equipment or furniture that you use for the business.
- Current assets – anything that you sell.
- Debtors – anyone that owes you money should be included in here. If you offer accounts or sell to clients who settle monthly, then include sums owed in this column.
- Current liabilities – anything that you owe that is payable within one year. In our list we have included creditors – which might include your suppliers as you will typically pay them in around 30 days – and the overdraft as this is probably repayable on demand.
- Net current assets – this is simply the sum of your current assets and liabilities both of which are likely to be under one year in lifespan. This is quite a useful figure to calculate as it will show whether you could pay all your debts if you collected all the sums due to you.
- Total Assets less Current Liabilities – unlike the last number you can include all the long-term assets like property in this number.
- Equity – any money that is invested in the business, for example your savings if you used those to set up the business initially.

Profit and loss (P&L) sheet

Put simply, a profit and loss sheet details your business' transactions, subtracting the total outgoings from the total income to give you a reading of how much, if any, profit you have made.

> **TIP**
>
> A profit and loss sheet, unlike a balance sheet, displays the financial health of your company for a period of time – a month, a quarter or a year. A balance sheet only represents your finances at a particular moment in time.

If your company is incorporated, you are required by law to produce a P&L sheet for each financial year. If your shop is not trading as a limited company you don't have to produce one, but the information you give to HMRC to work out your tax bill will amount to the same thing anyway. Even if you're not required to produce one, the P&L sheet is useful to show owners, investors and shareholders how the business is doing at a glance.

You can find an example shop P&L sheet on page 83.

➡ CASHFLOW STATEMENT

A cashflow statement shows your shop's incoming and outgoing money, enabling you to assess how much money you have at your disposal at any one time. Poor cashflow is one of the number one causes for businesses to fail. Some businesses can be profitable on paper, earning more than their outgoings, but if the cash isn't in the bank to buy stock and the pay staff you'll soon find yourself in trouble. Providing you continue to take a high percentage of cash payments you should stay relatively cashflow positive.

Having said that, your first few months are the time you're most likely to run into difficulties with cashflow. A lot more money will have been spent by you – on premises, initial stock, equipment, staff – than the first few customers will pay you for their purchases, so on paper you'll be cashflow negative. There are certain things businesses can do to increase their cashflow and the most obvious is to ask their customers to pay them quicker. Shops can't really do that but here's a few things you can do to improve cashflow:

- Lease rather than buy the really expensive equipment you need. You'll then pay a monthly or annual charge rather than having to splash out all at once.
- Order less stock – don't order too many of the items that will sit in your stockroom for months before hitting the shelves.
- Make sure you forecast your cashflow as accurately as you can. That way you can plan ahead for slower revenue periods and make sure you still have enough cash in the bank to cover your outgoings.

Paul Mathers, Sherston Post Office Stores

Different weeks in a month present different problems. If you have two large accounts to pay at one time on top of PAYE and VAT, the impact on cashflow can be massive. I always keep £5,000 in the account to accommodate for month end payments.

Cashflow forecasting

Good cashflow forecasting isn't just important for your own business management. You may be required to provide this kind of detail if you need a loan from the bank during your first few months of trading. The forecast will allow you to identity the amount and origin of cash coming into your business and the amount and destination of cash being paid out during any given period of time.

Generally you'll produce a forecast for a quarter or year in advance, but during the early stages of trading you might want to do this more frequently, such as a month in advance. When compiling a cashflow forecast it's really important that you don't overestimate your incoming cash.

TIP

It's much easier to get an accurate reflection of your outgoings as you will know what these are at this stage. However, you won't yet have a really accurate estimate of how many customers you'll have each month, so err on the side of caution to be safe and keep your incoming cash estimates low.

VAT

VAT or Value Added Tax applies to the majority of transactions involving the sale of goods or services. Once your business reaches a certain level of turnover, currently £67,000 per year, you are legally obliged to register for VAT. You will then have to apply VAT to what you sell and keep records of you incomings and outgoings in order to pay the correct amount of VAT to HMRC.

To register for VAT go to the VAT Online Registration Service on the HMRC website.

There are three rates of VAT:

1. The standard rate – 17.5%
2. The reduced rate – 5%
3. The zero rate – 0%

TIP

If you find the prospect of dealing with VAT daunting don't worry. You can appoint an agent – accountant, bookkeeper or tax advisor – to deal with it on your behalf by registering them on HMRC's VAT Online Registration Service.

It's really important you register for VAT in good time because otherwise you will liable for all VAT due from the time that you should have been registered. In other words you have to pay HMRC the right amount of VAT even if you didn't charge your customers for it. You could also be liable to pay a fine for delaying your registration. How much you'll be fined is dependent on how late you registered, but fines start at £50.

The average time for processing VAT applications is about one month, however, it can take up to six months if HMRC feels it needs to carry out extra checks on the application. You must account for and pay VAT between applying for your registration and receiving your actual VAT number, but you are also allowed to reclaim any VAT you have paid suppliers on your purchases during this point. To do this you need to keep accurate records of any invoices where your suppliers have charged you VAT.

➡ THE DAY TO DAY

Price changes

Contrary to popular belief it's not just sales that affect profitability but costs, and your outgoings will change, sometimes on a weekly basis. The price of products and the cost of energy are variable and may go up and down frequently. While customers accept inflation as a fact of life, they'll start to cry foul play if your products have jumped in price every time they visit your shop. Consequently you need to find a balance between covering your own costs and maintaining reasonable prices for your customer.

One way of doing this is to set yourself a variable acceptable mark-up. For example, calculate what the lowest possible mark-up for an acceptable return is (eg 60%) then the highest mark-up you can reasonably expect to charge (70%). This gives you some leeway for price changes for your own costings without leaving you out of pocket for not passing the cost on to your customers. However, when your own costs go up so much that it's no longer possible to make at least the 60% mark-up, that's when you'll need to change your prices.

Managing cash payments

Although you'll want to retain some cash from each day's takings to make up the next till float, it's not a good idea to keep lots of cash on the premises, especially if you don't have a secure safe at the shop. However, as you're likely to be open long after the banks shut you almost certainly should have one; or you'll need to make some provision for storing cash safely before you can deposit it. Fit your safe inside locked rooms, away from exits and ideally planted within a wall.

> ### TIP
> Try not to go more than a day without taking cash to the bank, but avoid making deposits at the same time each day. Also, it's important to vary your route so you don't become an easy target for thieves that see you walking to the bank regularly.

The float

Increasingly people prefer to pay by plastic (credit or debit cards) but good old-fashioned cash is still king and in times of economic downturn as we've seen this year, there's a tendency to revert to paying with what's in your purse.

As a result you need to make sure you have a float for each day so that change can be given out. It's a good idea to keep at least £200 in various notes, including as many £5 notes as possible. These can be hard to come by and are given out in change more than you're likely to receive them. You may find you need to get some from the bank if you don't have a large enough supply. You'll also need plenty of pound coins and smaller denominations as you're likely to give some change back with nearly every cash payment.

Cheque and credit card payments

Cheques are still used by some, but many shops are now refusing to accept them for a number of reasons. Firstly, they generally take longer to clear than credit card payments, which can have an adverse affect on your cashflow. Secondly, there's no instant notification about whether the payment has been accepted, and unless your customer has used a cheque guarantee card, you may find yourself with the odd bounced cheque.

Without doubt you need to take credit and debit card payments and there's more on getting merchant status in the Getting Legal section. You need to be meticulous about your record-keeping and storing of receipts. It'll cost you between 2%–6% to accept a credit card payment. This will vary according to your bank and merchant account, but don't pass this on as a surcharge to your customer as it only acts as an incentive not to buy.

➡ ACCOUNTANTS

Even some of the most mathematically-minded entrepreneurs will tell you a good accountant can be worth their weight in gold. You're a shopkeeper first and foremost and as I said at the beginning of the chapter that's where your passion should remain, not getting bogged down with invoices, PAYE slips and credit notes. Handing that responsibility over to an accountant or someone who completely manages your books can free up your time to spend on planning, development and working on your grand designs for the future of your shop and retail empire.

FROM THE EXPERTS:
Mike Clare, Dreams plc

Running a small business, especially a shop, involves a degree of multi-tasking but you can't be good at everything. Get an accountant because a good one will save you money.

Choosing an accountant

When you're just starting out, your accountant can act as one of your most valued business advisors so you need to make sure you employ one that you trust. There are many ways to find a good accountant and one of the best methods is through a recommendation. Ask friends and contacts if they would recommend their accountant. Also ask businesses around you if they go to someone locally.

> ### ✦ TIP
>
> Your solicitor or bank manager may also be able to recommend an accountant, or if not a particular person they should be able to point you in the right direction for an accountancy firm that specialises in the retail sector and has experience of working with small independent shops and start-ups.

When seeking recommendations, make sure you ask people what they used their accountant for as you might not need the same kind of service. Ask what in particular they recommend about them and what their weak points are if they have any. Most importantly it is advisable to choose someone who is a member of one of the main professional accounting bodies. There is no legislation to stop anyone setting up as an accountant so asking for member accountants in your area will ensure you are getting someone fully qualified.

> These are the main accounting organisations in the UK:
>
> Association of Chartered Certified Accountants
> Tel: 020 7059 5000
> www.acca.org.uk
>
> Institute of Chartered Accountants, Scotland
> Tel: 0131 347 0100
> www.icas.org.uk
>
> Institute of Chartered Accountants, England and Wales
> Tel: 020 7920 8100
> www.icaew.co.uk

Remember you're likely to be working closely with your accountant and if you don't get on at a basic level, your professional relationship may be more difficult than it needs to be. If you find someone you think you like ask if you can speak to their other clients. This is like asking for references and will be a real test of the calibre of the firm or individual accountant. If they are confident that their service has impressed, they shouldn't have a problem referring you to a few people.

Accounting software

If you decide you're going to manage the books yourself you'll want to get yourself some accountancy software. Whoever's job it is, yours or an accountant's, the person balancing the books, chasing invoices, managing suppliers and paying staff doesn't need to be worrying about the latest technology and it's probably the last thing on their mind. However, buying an accountancy software package can slash the amount of time and effort you put into managing your finances.

From reminders for chasing payment to generating invoices, a good package is like a virtual accounts department. It can tell you how much you are owed and by whom; how long it takes you to pay your bills; what you have in stock and what you have in the bank at any moment in time. More importantly, it could also give you those vital breakdowns of how much you are making on each service, day or month. Of course, there's nothing stopping you or your accountant working from a basic Excel spreadsheet, but bear in mind that a good accountancy software package can drastically reduce your accounting bill every year.

There are plenty of packages out there, each tailored to the size and type of business being run. You can also choose a package that links up to your EPOS system if you have one, which we have already covered in Decking It Out.

When choosing a package consider the following before you buy:

- Value for money – what services do you get for your buck?
- Level of support – does the package include a free helpline you can call for technical or set-up support?
- Is the software industry specific?
- Does it integrate easily with HMRC's online filing system? This can save you a lot of time when it comes to filing your returns.

➡ PAYING YOUR STAFF

Shops often have a lot of casual and temporary staff, and it can be tempting to just pay them cash at the end of each week or shift. However, it's your responsibility as an employer to make sure the payment of your staff is all above board and both they and your business are making the appropriate tax and national insurance contributions.

PAYE

PAYE (Pay As You Earn) is HMRC's system for collecting income tax and National Insurance at the source of payment – ie before the employee receives it. It's your responsibility to make sure you know how much to deduct from your staff in terms of their personal tax requirements. You must send the deducted amounts to HMRC by the 19th of every month (or the 22nd if you make electronic payments). However, if monthly payments are under £1,500 you can do this on a quarterly basis.

You have three choices when it comes to organising PAYE. You can either keep written accounts and calculate tax and National Insurance deductions yourself, buy specialised software to help calculate it for you, or outsource the whole operation.

PAYE is applied to all payments your employees receive when working for you. This includes:

- Wages
- Overtime
- Tips
- Bonuses
- Statutory sick pay
- Statutory maternity / paternity / adoption pay
- Any lump sums including redundancy payments

Once again, a quick visit to the HMRC website will allow you to register your business for PAYE. You should have already done this before employing your first member of staff, but if you haven't done so already, give the HMRC's New Employer Hotline a call on 0845 60 70 143 and order a New Employer Starter Pack. This will talk you through the basics of registering.

Staff records

There are three main types of documentation to give your staff so they have a record of what they've earned and how much income tax and National Insurance they've paid. These are:

- Wage slips – this shows how much they've earned and how it has been calculated
- P60 form – this shows the tax deducting during the whole tax year. You can order this from HMRC by calling the Employers Orderline on 0845 7646 646
- P45 – you only need to give your employees this when they stop working for you. It will contain their individual tax code which they need to pass on to their new employer

Outsourcing payroll

Many shops decide to outsource their payroll duties so they don't have to calculate tax and National Insurance deductions themselves. This will obviously be an added expense for your business but can save you a lot of time and money in the long-run. By outsourcing your payroll you get rid of one of the biggest administrative headaches of running a small business.

If you have an accountant, they should be able to provide you with advice on outsourcing your payroll, and may even by able to do it for you. As with any service, shop around for the best deal as much as time permits.

Before you decide on an outsourced payroll provider, make sure you consider the following:

- Are they used to dealing with shops?
- Do they supply monthly or weekly pay slips? (You may find weekly slips are more suited for casual staff.)
- How much will they charge for setting up your payroll system?
- What are the ongoing fees?
- How easy is it to add extra members of staff to the account?
- Is the software they use approved by HMRC?

Things to remember:

- Be thorough in your record-keeping. The better organised your figures are, the better your organised your shop will be.

- Be cautious in your forecasting. It's better to underestimate trade than overestimate.

- Make sure you register for VAT in good time to avoid HMRC delay fines.

- Don't try to manage it all yourself if you don't have the time or skills. Hire an accountant if you need one.

- Consider outsourcing your payroll but carry out the appropriate checks before handing the process over to a third party.

Management of staff and yourself

There's simply no avoiding the fact that a shop is nothing without the service provided by the people running it. Unfortunately, while it's not hard to find people, it is difficult, especially in retail where staff turnover is at its highest, to keep hold of good staff members.

To do that, and to keep your team motivated and bringing in the sales that keep your business healthy, you'll need to be familiar with the qualities of effective leadership and develop a management style that works. When evaluating your team of staff you'll have to consider not just problems like theft but also if they could benefit from any training or if there are any benefits you could offer to motivate them. From employee number one, you'll also need to start keeping abreast of the myriad that is HR legislation.

In this chapter we'll cover:

- How to manage yourself
- When to take advice
- Time management and holidays
- Employing a manager
- Managing staff
- Dealing with staff problems
- HR issues
- Staff benefits

➡ MANAGING YOURSELF

The minute you employ another person you go from being a humble shop owner to a boss, a manager and the point from which authority and company culture flows. If you're not used to it, that can be quite a culture shock. Some people react by becoming too authoritarian, others try too hard not to change and end up losing respect. To run a motivated, disciplined workforce you'll need to strike a balance between the two and lead by example.

Taking advice

We covered the value of taking advice from others in Before You Start, but it's important to remember this is not something you should forget about once you're up and running. Mentors and established entrepreneurs can have something to offer your business even if it's a decade old. It's always good to have an outsider's perspective that may be able to tell you where your strengths lie, and which areas of the business or management you're neglecting.

Once you've established yourself as a shop owner you may find people more willing to confide and share with you as you can offer them advice in return. Networking should be an ongoing process. Try and mix with other shop owners at industry and local events, where you can share experiences and seek support.

Also, don't rule out general free business networking events such as Startupslive, details of which can be found at www.startupslive.co.uk. These types of events bring together entrepreneurs from all kinds of industries, and you never know when a contact you make will come in useful. As a shop owner you mustn't think that only other shop owners can offer useful advice or guidance. Running a shop shares the same principles of running any kind of business and you'll be surprised at how friendly and open to communication people can be when they share the same goals as you.

> **FROM THE EXPERTS:**
> ## John Spooner, Monsoon
>
> Running a business can feel like a lonely experience, and it can sometimes feel like you put up with a lot of shit for little reward. But you're not alone and sharing with other entrepreneurs can really help. Experience is especially good to listen to especially if that person has encountered the same situations in the past.

Identifying your strengths and weaknesses

As a business owner you develop and hone your skills everyday. However, if you want to maintain a successful business, you have to dedicate just as much time to your own self-development as to your shop.

It can be hard to measure your own personal development when you're your own boss. Just because your shop turns over a tidy sum at the end of each month, doesn't mean you're as effective as you can be as a leader. That's where the focussed and planned development of your knowledge and skills through training can benefit you.

Running a shop, much like running any other kind of small business, requires you to be multi-skilled. The role of shop owner can involve everything from buying stock, dealing with customers, creative store design, business planning and taking care of the accounts. Regardless of whether you have a hands-on position in all of these roles you need to be at least familiar with what they entail.

If you employ a shop manager or even assistant with more retail experience than you and see them following certain processes, swallow your pride and ask them about it. They'll appreciate you showing an interest and you'll get valuable insight. Ask questions of your accountant. You may not be a whizz with numbers but you still need to understand the basics of a tax form or balance sheet. You might feel silly asking something a GCSE business studies students knows after term one, but you'll never know unless you ask and who ever asked you to be an expert in everything, anyway?

If you can't afford an army of experts to staff your shop with, then take advantage of the help available to you. Contact your local Regional Development Agency (www.englandsrdas.com), or visit a Business Link (www.businesslink.gov.uk) advisor. They can point you in the right direction to what's on offer in terms of training. Many courses are free for small business owners, so you can't even use lack of funds as an excuse.

The industry moves fast. What's en vogue for shop décor one month may seem passé half a year down the line. You need to keep up to date with the latest shop trends and fashions. Subscribe to trade magazines and websites and visit trade shows. You'll be surprised at what you can get out of them – new ideas, inspiration and a wealth of new contacts, possible suppliers or even customers.

> **FROM THE EXPERTS:**
> ## John Spooner, Monsoon
>
> Know your limitations. Some entrepreneurs are better off left in the office. If your skills don't align with the front of the house, get a good floor manager.

Motivating yourself

The fact that you've even chosen to start a shop suggests you're an incredibly motivated person, but once the doors have opened and the regular customers start to flock, how can you make sure you maintain that level of enthusiasm? The start-up process is incredibly demanding both physically and psychologically. After all that hard work you clearly need to slow down the pace slightly, but you can't sit back and hope the shop will run itself.

In the same way you might set targets for staff, and KPIs (key performance indicators) to measure performance and flag training and resource needs, you need to do the same for yourself.

If you see you're not performing as you'd like, take stock. Don't be too harsh on yourself though, it'll almost certainly be a case that you're doing too much and need to delegate more.

Again, sharing experiences and networking can keep you motivated. Being a shop owner, as with running any business, can be a lonely experience where you're expected to shoulder all the responsibility. Having people to share that with you can really lift the load, reassure you you're not alone and replenish your determination.

More than anything though, make sure you appreciate what you have achieved as well as what's left to do.

Time management

With so many hats to wear in your role as shop owner, managing your time effectively is absolutely essential and is where many people fall down. It's absolutely critical that you grasp the principles of strong time management from a very early stage.

The most important aspect of time management is to list and prioritise everything you need to do. This will allow you to recognise the difference between what's important and what's urgent. Running a shop will involve various 'to do' lists. There's your long-term goals such as growing turnover and improving your margins, nurturing and expanding your customer base and developing your own skills as a business owner.

Next come your monthly goals, which could be introducing a new product range, recruiting new sales assistants, finding a new supplier or getting your accounts in order. And of course there'll be daily and weekly objectives – stocktaking ahead of a cash 'n' carry trip, changing the store layout or window design and sorting the payroll.

If you're running certain types of shops, certain times of the day will be busier than others and dictate when you can and can't focus on administrative or planning responsibilities.

Whatever your role within the actual shop opening times, you need to set aside enough time to get on with these tasks as they are just as important as serving customers when it comes to running a successful establishment.

Here are a few tips for prioritising workloads and making sure you don't neglect important aspects of running your business:

- List all the tasks you need to do, and then prioritise them in order of what is most urgent and important.
- Don't underestimate the amount of time interruptions can steal from your schedule. When allocating time for a particular task, build in room for disruptions.
- Don't be afraid to turn off your phone or email and ask not to be disturbed when you really need to concentrate. If having no distractions helps you get a task done more quickly, you may end up with extra time to deal with clients, customers or staff.
- Break large tasks up into manageable chunks. It's tempting to run lots of little errands instead of getting stuck in to a big important job. However, completing it one stage at a time will make it seem less daunting.
- Build room into your schedule for unexpected problems or events. If nothing unforeseen crops up, you'll end up ahead of schedule.
- Make sure no more than half your time is allocated to top priority work. All those little jobs that aren't as time sensitive will start to mount up if you don't crack on with them.
- If possible, delegate. You may think the shop will fall apart if you don't oversee everything, but perhaps your time can be more valuably spent.

Holidays and work/life balance

Deciding when the right time to take a break is a tricky thing to master. On the one hand your shop will still be very much in its infancy at this stage. However, you will have worked incredibility hard to get the venture up and running and may feel in desperate need of a break by this point.

There's no specific right or wrong answer to when the best time to take a break or holiday is. At such an early stage in the company's life you may feel you simply can't afford to leave it in someone else's hands. The main thing to remember is that you need to achieve a balance between working hard to make sure the shop thrives during its early days, and making sure you don't burn out yourself. Working too hard without a break can be counterproductive and bad for your health. It's always best to take a breather before you get to the point where you simply can't keep up the pace.

If you do decide to take a break then test the waters first. Don't book two weeks in the sun without knowing for sure you've got a solid team in place to run things in your absence. Start by asking your second in command to open up one day, then lock up, then do both and go to the bank with the day's takings etc. Handing over the reins for a weekend while you're still close at hand, perhaps even just at home, is the next step.

By doing this you can test if things are capable of running smoothly in your absence while still being nearby if any real problems arise. It's actually a healthy situation to get into and the longer you leave it, the more you expose your business to real problems if something happens to you.

Once you're confident the whole operation won't collapse as soon as you've closed the door behind you, you'll find you have a far more rewarding break and can come back refreshed, raring to go, and hopefully full of new ideas for the shop.

Handing over the reins

Employing a manager to run the shop for you is a big step. Whether or not you do this from the outset will probably depend on how big your shop is. A smaller establishment can get by with sales assistants and a more senior member of the team. However, if it can't or if it was never your intention to be based on site full-time you'll need to get someone experienced and trustworthy in to manage day to day operations while you oversee strategy and high level decisions.

Before you even think about hiring a manager, you must be sure it's what you really want. You'll have to delegate a lot of responsibility and you'll run into problems if you're not willing to relinquish some control and allow the manger to have a degree of autonomy.

Be clear in your head about why you've decided to take someone on in this role. Are you just looking for someone to watch over the shop when you're not there, or are you handing over more responsibility than that? Will they be completely in charge of hiring and firing other staff? How much input will they have when it comes to products you stock and pricing?

It's so important to have all this worked out before you start recruiting as it will determine the type of person you're looking for, how much you're willing to pay them and what kind of relationship they'll have with both you and the other members of staff.

➡ MANAGING STAFF

No matter who you're managing you need to clearly outline and put down in writing what their role is, make it clear what you expect from them and demonstrate how their performance will be measured. You then need to ensure you set clear lines of communications, both from you to them and them to you, to flag and deal with any problems.

There's nothing worse than a boss who doesn't communicate what they expect then reprimands staff for not delivering it. Yet it's equally galling how many people are motivated to start their own business having been on the receiving end of such poor practice then only succeed in doing the same.

The best bosses are fair. They're firm but they listen and they apply the same rules to themselves as they do on the shopfloor. You should lead by example in every respect: dress smart, be punctual and have manners, be serious when it matters and have a sense of humour and fun when appropriate.

Despite this, there should always be a separation between you and the people that work for you. There's nothing stopping you getting on with your employees and even becoming friends, but keep a professional distance. It's far easier if things turn sour, stops resentment from other staff members and maintains a clearly defined structure where everyone knows their roles.

> **FROM THE EXPERTS:**
> **Mike Clare, Dreams plc**
>
> You have to lead from the front. You've got to smile even if you're tired, got a headache or had an argument with your wife, because you need to keep the mood in the shop right. You've got to be able to do anything the staff do. If they see you cleaning and hoovering they'll think, well if he's the boss and he does it there's no reason I shouldn't.

Staff training and courses

The shop industry is one where the most important techniques and principles are learned on the job. However, that doesn't mean you or store manager should be left with the responsibility of teaching everything. For example, if all your sales assistants would benefit from a course in innovative retail display or customer service, you should weigh up the cost of getting outside training. There are plenty of courses, most of which can be done in a day or less, which teach the fundamentals in any retail skill.

Why not dedicate a day where all, or at least half, the shop's staff can train together? This doesn't have to involve leaving the shop. Many courses involve a tutor or lecturer coming to you and doing on-site training.

Dealing with staffing problems

Most employers will experience difficulties with certain members of staff at various points in their career. The shop trade has high levels of staff turnover so keeping hold of staff that you trust and are dedicated and loyal to your business is no easy task. Unless you're extremely lucky, or only hire friends and family to work in the shop, it's likely you'll have to confront some of the following problems.

Theft

Unfortunately light fingers in the stock room is a relatively common problem and in some sections of retail are on a par with shoplifting. Some staff think the odd missing item will go unnoticed and won't make much difference to the bottom line. There's also the threat of till thefts to contend with. Any business that deals largely in cash transactions could fall victim to staff theft. And it's your profit that's walking out of the door, not turnover. If somebody is taking £10 a day on a turnover of £1,000 that's only 1% and you might think you can live with that. But if you're pulling in 6% profit (£60) on that £1,000, then thieves are taking one sixth of your profits. These losses need to be seen as a percentage of net profit not of gross turnover.

Although common in the shop business, there are steps you can take to reduce the prevalence of staff theft. The best place to start is with recruitment. Even if you're only employing part-timers, check their references. It's the casual staff that you need to pay the most attention to.

The next step is to explain to all members of staff the security controls that are operating in your business. Make sure everybody knows what will happen to them if they're caught stealing, then at the very least they can evaluate the risks involved before they pilfer.

You should also ensure the lines of authority and responsibility are clearly defined – staff need to know who they're responsible to and for. That way you stand a much better chance of a member of your team confiding in you if somebody is stealing.

It may be a tedious task but you also have to put in place systems that will alert you to possible staff theft problems. For example, you should be able to average out cashflow and sales over a week and over a month. This allows you to build up a picture of how much you should be taking on a Monday in September, say.

It's also a good idea not to hold too much cash in tills as it can be a temptation. You only really need to carry enough cash to give change from a £50 note, all the surplus notes should be removed regularly.

While it doesn't always go down well, it can also pay to do spot searches of staff bags before they leave although you can't do this without their permission.

If you do catch someone stealing, you'll almost certainly be within your rights to fire them for an act of gross misconduct. However, no matter how red-handed you've caught them and even if they've fully admitted the crime, if you don't follow the correct disciplinary procedure as explained in the Getting Legal channel, you could find yourself up in front of a tribunal. No matter how angry you might be, take a deep breath and follow the rule book – it's really not worth the hassle or the money.

Bad service, laziness and body language

Every customer that enters your shop should be important to you. That sounds like one of those annoying messages that you get on automated call systems that prove you don't matter quite enough to employ more staff to answer the phones. As such, it's no good just saying it, you have to provide a friendly and helpful atmosphere and provide a positive shopper experience every single minute over every single hour you're open, every single day of the year.

That's easier said than done when you're having a bad day, let alone when your 18-year-old shop assistant has been dumped by her boyfriend. Good customer service is something you can't relent on and you should never tolerate a slip in standards, no matter how frustrating or downright awkward the customer. It doesn't matter if the customer is right or wrong if they go away and tell 20 people your shop is rubbish.

When recruiting look for natural enthusiasm and people skills, it's generally something you can't teach unlike other skills. Encourage your staff to be enthusiastic but not too imposing. There's a fine line between being friendly and being annoying. Body language should reflect a willingness to attend and help, and should convey that they're approachable while not overbearing or loitering.

Appearances are also important. Uniforms are a good idea and encourage staff to arrive dressed ready to start work, especially if they arrive through the front of the shop. If you don't require your staff to wear a uniform then make sure you set certain standards in the dress code from the outset. It can be difficult to tell people what they're wearing isn't suitable if you haven't given any guidance on clothing in the first place.

Discrimination

We've already touched on the issue of discrimination during the Recruiting Staff chapter but it's important to note that this is something you must constantly bear in mind. There's plenty more detail on how to comply with discrimination laws on Startups.co.uk but to summarise, you must consider the following legislation in the day to day running of your shop or you could find yourself in serious hot water.

Legislation outlawing age discrimination came into force in 2006. It includes every member of staff that works for you, both young and old. Employers must have age positive practises. This means you can't recruit, train, promote or retire people on the basis of age unless it can be objectively justified. Many people over 50 want to work but are prevented from doing so by ageist practices. But remember, the recent legislation doesn't just concern older people; it covers young and old alike throughout their working lives.

Skills, experience and the ability to do the job are what's important, not someone's age. However, the legislation doesn't just have advantages for employees. As a shop owner, stamping out age discrimination can have a positive effect on staff turnover, higher morale, lower recruitment costs, better productivity and increased profits.

The same applies when it comes to discriminating on the grounds of race, sex or disability. It's your responsibility to make sure that not only do you treat all your staff equally, but that discrimination does not take place between other members of the team.

Discrimination can take many forms, and it's not just a case of refusing to hire someone for being a woman/gay/ 65 years old. There's also indirect discrimination, where certain members are denied opportunities within employment, experience harassment such as unwanted advances or comments of a sexual nature, or bullying.

If somebody working for you is a victim of any of these kinds of discrimination you could find yourself fighting in an employment tribunal, which is costly in terms of time, reputation and turnover.

Staff handbook

In an industry with such a high rate of staff turnover, you may have staff that only last a few months or even weeks at your shop. While you need to make sure every member of staff has the appropriate training in health and safety, some of the other expectations of employee policy can be detailed in a staff handbook. Here you can list your expectations of all staff and your policy on issues such as theft, absence, dress code and general working attitude. That way if a problem ever arises you can refer back to the handbook as an explanation of why you may be taking disciplinary action.

However, you should also use the handbook as a way of flagging up staff benefits and the elements of your shop that you think are the advantages of working there.

What goes in a staff handbook?

Your staff handbook should cover your policy on:

- Company morals or ethos
- Dress code
- Dealing with customers
- Absence and lateness procedure
- What day of the week or month salaries are paid
- Holiday entitlement
- Any bonus or reward schemes
- Health and safety procedures

Staff benefits

Thinking about the extra perks which can make your shop stand out as a great place to work compared to the many other establishments your staff may have experienced can reduce your staff turnover.

Here are a few examples of the kind of things you can do for your staff to encourage loyalty and hard work:

- Offer exclusive in-store discounts
- Incentivise staff with individual and team commissions based on a percentage of sales for the shop per day and on a monthly basis
- Encourage team spirit with after work drinks or activities
- Offer bonuses or gifts for staff that never miss a shift or turn up late, or just generally as a reward for hard work and enthusiasm

- Celebrate birthdays or special occasions – this could be in the form of a toast or even something as simple a card signed by all the other members of the team
- Offer extra benefits for long-term service. Offering an extra day's holiday per year of service can be far more cost effective then going through the same recruitment process every couple of months
- Offer regular appraisals and give staff the opportunity to discuss any issues they want to raise. There may not be time during normal shifts to talk about problems or ask questions. Make sure you're approachable when staff really need you to listen

Things to remember:

- Take advice as and when you need it, whatever stage in your shop career.

- Set goals for effect time management, taking breaks when you need them.

- Learn to delegate. You can't do everything on your own.

- Be fair but authoritative, and make sure all your managers are the same.

- Reward good work wherever possible. An atmosphere where staff are only singled out when they do something wrong breeds bad morale.

Ongoing marketing

Y ou've overcome the first hurdle by getting those first few customers through the door. Perhaps you hosted an extravagant launch party that made the local papers, or got a few celebrity guests seen in your shop. The tricky process is making sure you stay in the forefront of your customers' minds. It's no good if they come in once, leave relatively impressed then don't come back again. You want repeat custom, and a constant supply of brand new customers too. This is where your ongoing marketing comes in.

This chapter will help you determine what your marketing plan should be and what kinds of marketing work best for you. This could include promotions to help increase business, such as the good old buy-one-get-one-free offer, or discounts on a certain range of goods. There is also advice on how to get your shop into a variety of listings and guides, including online, so your customers know what you offer and where to find you.

In this chapter we'll cover:

- What marketing is
- How to form your own marketing strategy
- How to measure the success of your marketing plan
- Ideas for offers and promotions

- Advertising and PR
- Getting into shopping guides and business directories
- How to market your business online

➡ WHAT IS MARKETING?

Marketing isn't just advertising. It's the means by which your shop identifies, attracts, and keeps its customers; and that's such a powerful proposition it touches on almost every other element of your business. If carried out effectively it will not only ensure that your shop is seen and heard but will give it the flexibility to adapt to changing customer demands in an ever-evolving business environment.

Marketing will help you understand who your customers are, what they aspire to and how you can position your shop as the destination they're looking for. It'll influence your buying decisions, how you price items, what packaging you use, the level of customer service you provide and the area you look to next if you open a second shop.

Successful marketing is about accumulating knowledge and is an art as well as a science. You should be collecting knowledge from every day's trade and every transaction and purchase you make should influence the next one, as well as govern how you try and promote yourself.

While your shop started off as your baby, for it to grow and achieve its full potential you'll have to allow your customers to dictate which direction it takes. You won't be able to do that, or bring in more like them, if you're not fully knowledgeable about who they are and what they want.

But you shouldn't find the process daunting, keeping up with the changing demands of customers and finding new ways to get them through your doors is to be embraced. If you've a great shop offering they want and know how to flaunt it, then marketing can be one of the most enjoyable elements of running a shop.

> **FROM THE EXPERTS:**
> **John Spooner, Monsoon**
>
> Word of mouth is very powerful. John Lewis spend very little on advertising because they believe in the power of happy satisfied customers.

Marketing plans

There are no hard and fast rules for creating a marketing strategy. It's up to you to set your own goals. However, as a general rule, you need to ask what you want your shop to achieve in a year, two years or even five years' time compared to where it would be without a marketing strategy.

Here are some tips to remember when devising your marketing plan:

- Start by setting clear objectives – where do you want your shop to go?
- Set clear financial targets for these objectives.
- Define your target market and identify your potential customers.
- Decide on the brand and the values you want to communicate.
- Plan your promotion strategy.
- Set a budget.
- Devise a schedule.
- Decide how the strategy will be measured, for example, increased sales, direct responses, coverage in local press etc.
- Implement the programme according to the schedule.
- Monitor and evaluate results as an aid for future marketing decisions.

Measuring success

If you've got several marketing or PR strategies happening at once it can be difficult to measure which ones are actually bringing in the customers. You're not going to advertise in a newspaper and then ask each customer that walks through the door if they've popped in because they saw an advert in the local rag. If you're not sure which marketing technique is giving you the best return on investment then why not try them one by one, then calculate any increase in customers or turnover for that period.

Of course the success of certain promotions, such as vouchers or discounts using codes are easy enough to measure because you can count up how many customers make use of the offers. However it's important to remember that you need to bring in more custom as a result of the promotion than you spend on your marketing. It's no good offering discounts and double your footfall if you end up making a loss on your products.

For each piece of marketing you do, set clear KPIs (key performance indicators) that will help you assess if it's proved worthwhile.

Promotional ideas

One way of attracting new customers is to run special offers or promotions. Shops traditionally have end of season sales, but there are other ways to incentivise people off the street:

Loss leaders

Covered in Your First Six Months, loss leaders are items you sell at cost price to tempt customers into the premises so they'll buy other items that are priced to give you the same overall profit.

Buy one get one free (BOGOF)

BOGOFs are now staple retail fodder. However beware that you could cheapen a product by offering on such a deal or even set the wrong tone for your brand – and make sure you can afford to give away a whole unit for free. Chances are you won't find it as easy as the supermarkets do.

Limited special offers

Daily or weekly offers keep the shop looking fresh and feel like you're offering an incentive or weekly special more than trying to sell off stock that's out of season or end of line.

Loyalty cards

While the Boots and Nectar card are more about collecting customer buying habits, simple loyalty cards can work as a way of attracting return customers. If your pricing allows you to, offer discounts or freebies after certain thresholds of expenditure or per X number of visits.

Competitions

A great way to collect customer data is to offer in store competitions. Offer an attractive prize and get customers to enter by filling in their details on a slip. You can then email and mail them all thanking them for entering and offering a call to action incentive – £5 off or 10% discount etc – to get them back.

More launches

Don't miss the chance to get your top customers and the press back for a drink (and shop, of course). If you start stocking a new range or brand of goods, run a preview night, promote it in the window and contact your customer base. It's amazing how far a few bottles of plonk can go.

Partnerships

Seek out mutually-beneficial partnerships with complimentary shops or organisations. For instance, if you run a florists contact wedding organisers and funeral directors and promote each other's services. Look to local clubs, groups and companies used by your target customer and ask if you can put a poster up or distribute promotional material in exchange for providing them with a small discount. You'll find most will welcome this as a way of attracting members or employees.

Keep an eye on your diary and what's going on around you. If there's a bandwagon you can jump on, leap on it. If your town or local community is campaigning for an issue dear to your customers' hearts, put a poster in your window. If you can help local schools, help them. React to festivities and celebrations. It should go without saying, for instance, if you're running an off-license, Guinness should be in your front window for St. Patrick's Day and champagne for Valentine's Day.

> ### FROM THE EXPERTS:
> ### Mike Clare, Dreams plc
>
> Create your own PR. We used to open for 24 hours and get the managers and their partners to sleep in the front window. No one buys anything but you generate publicity.

➡ ADVERTISING VS PR

We've already discussed advertising in The Opening, but it's important to consider the value of continuing to advertise. While initial advertising campaigns are good for informing customers that may not walk past your shop of its presence, ongoing advertising can be great for flagging up promotions or new lines. However, this early on in your shop's life, you may not yet be breaking even, let alone have enough profits set aside to spend on advertising. That's where PR can prove the most effective route for promotion.

You may have had coverage in a local papers or magazines when you launched but how do you keep the PR momentum going once you've been open a few months? Hopefully you've more than one story to tell, so you can keep churning out the press releases. Remember, for everything that happens to your business and every new line your shop stocks, try and think of a newsworthy angle for it.

Another interesting way of getting your shop some free coverage in a local paper is to offer up your services to them. Offer them a competition to win a £100 voucher to spend with you – even if you did it once a week chances are it'd still work out cheaper than buying an ad and £100 at sale value shouldn't be a £100 at cost value.

IN MY EXPERIENCE:
Clare Thommen, Boudiche

If you want PR you have to make yourself available and can't let it slip. PR is difficult to measure and is a long-term hit but it's worth it.

See if you can help out a paper or magazine by writing a column or advisory piece as a local shop owner or as an expert in your specialist area. Mock up an example and send it in. Don't make it too hard sell and, as many welcome free contributions, they might run it as a regular feature giving your shop a nice plug in exchange.

Forming media relationships

There are plenty of ways to get free coverage but you have to make sure you're not a nuisance to the journalists that you need to write about you. Here are some tips for getting the media on your side:

- Invite them round to the shop and buy them lunch to find out how you can get provide content they want. If you've met and spoken to them face-to-face they're far more likely to give you the time of day later on.
- Don't contact them too often. If you become a nuisance they may just start avoiding you.
- Don't contact them with irrelevant stories. It's important you tailor any press releases, stories or promotions to fit in with their publications and what their readers want to see.
- Find out when their deadline day is. If you contact a journalist when they're about to go to press they're unlikely to have time for you. Find out when their

publication goes out and contact them straight afterwards as this will be the time they're most likely to listen you.

- Write a good press release. Journalists receive endless quantities of them so you'll need to make yours stand out if you want a chance of it being read, let alone covered. Have a look at the Marketing and PR channel of Startups.co.uk for more details on how to write a winning press release.

- Ask magazines and newspaper supplements for forward features' lists so you can see if your journalists will be writing about an area that's particularly relevant to your shop.

➡ LISTINGS AND GUIDES

Getting yourself listed in a local directory doesn't have to cost anything. Most directories such as Thomson or the Yellow Pages will allow you to have a basic entry with the name of the shop the address and phone number for free. If you want a bigger advert with more prominence you will have to pay, however, you can expect to get a free trial for the paid-for premium services even if it means you pay for one month and get another free.

There are other smaller and more regularly updated local guides and directories which are often put through letterboxes or left in public buildings such as doctors' surgeries, information centres or local authority properties. These come in both printed and online formats. The printed guides or directories will have details on how to get your shop listed within them. Online versions will also have details of how to list for free or how to pay for greater prominence. Examples include, thebestof.co.uk, Welovelocal.com and Toplocallistings.co.uk.

⚓ TIP

Another site you may want to have your shop featured on is TrustedPlaces.com, a social networking site where members of the public put up personal reviews of restaurants, bars and shops they've visited and recommended. The shops featured then build up a ranking as voted for by the public.

There are plenty of other online review and listings sites dedicated to the retail industry. It's a good idea to check out the ones specific to your area and make sure you're listed on all of those too.

⇒ ONLINE MARKETING

My personal belief is that almost any shop can now supplement their income by selling online, whether it's through eBay or with their own website. Selling online is now so simple and cheap that the cost of getting a site up and running, can be easily recouped. While convenience stores and newsagents stand out as one large section of retail that e-commerce doesn't work for, many non-traditional web retailers are now enjoying success. For instance, Mitesh Soma's Chemist Direct is doing phenomenally well since launching in November 2007 and looks set to lead the way in massive changes in the way we buy pharmaceutical goods.

If you're not ready to sell online, at least get a website that promotes your shop and details its address, opening hours and contact details. Nearly half of small businesses still have no online presence despite the fact that there's a whole generation of people out there who find almost all their information online. For a basic site, you don't even have to pay for it, and can have it up and running in a couple of hours. There are a number of free services out there such as Microsoft's Office Live, or BT's Tradespace, which give you a free site which you can create and update yourself as often as you want.

> ✦ **TIP**
>
> Visit www.smallbusiness.officelive.com or www.bttradespace.com and get yourself an instant web presence without spending a single penny.

Web design

While these kind of services are great for giving you a basic web presence, if you want something a bit more flashy you'll probably need to get the professionals on board. It's not enough for your website to have a catchy domain name and some interesting content. People need to be instantly engaged when they land on a page, and much of that will stem from design, layout and how easy it is to navigate between, and find, different content.

Depending on the size and scope of your shop you may find you don't need to hire expensive web designers when you first get started. Bear in mind that your domain name is just an address, and you can change the look and feel of your site as many times as you want. Basically you'll want to strike a balance between a site that looks good, gets users to return and doesn't cost the earth to build.

Shop around for the best deal, perhaps even get companies to tender for the job based on a list of your requirements.

Make sure the design, feel and content on your website is in line with the brand and identity of your business. Make sure your target customer would feel at home there and feel like it's a place they'd enjoy visiting. Much as you did when designing your shop, visit competitors and complementary companies' websites and see what you can pick up.

Showcase what you sell, but make the website about you and your shop as well. Have a page that talks about why you started-up, what you hope to achieve and how passionate and determined you are to provide a great service.

Try and keep the site updated daily, perhaps carry relevant news and definitely write a blog where you talk about life in the shop and activity in your specialist area. It'll bring visitors to the site and place you as an expert in your field.

Collect visitor information wherever possible. Run competitions, ask people to sign up to receive special offers and use that data to provide a weekly or monthly newsletter telling them what's new in the shop and prompting them to visit. Use this marketing tool sparingly though. Customers don't want to be inundated with junk mail.

Things to remember:

- Have a clear and defined marketing strategy before you start spending your budget.

- Think carefully about what kind of promotions you offer and apply them to your slower days or times.

- Use PR sparingly but effectively. Don't become a nuisance to journalists.

- Look for strategic partnerships.

- Get yourself some web presence. However basic it is, you must be online in some form.

544,00

4.542,48
660,34
800,00   0,00
594,44   0,00

Business development

Business development

I f it's your ambition to rival a retail empire like Marks & Spencer's or Philip Green's Arcadia Group then who am I to stop you? That said, I'm guessing most of you will be more interested on getting shop number one open than thinking ahead to numbers 10, 100 or 1,000. For plenty of you, one shop will always be more than enough.

However, whether you're plotting to go empire building or stay happy one-shop bands for life, there will hopefully come a time when your business is sufficiently established to consider growing it. That might be as simple as diversifying its product range or sales channels or setting out on aggressive plan to roll-out your brand.

Either way it always pays to have one eye on the future, some would argue even as far ahead as when and how you'll stop running the business. As such, this chapter will explore all your business development options, from opening a second store to franchising and eventually selling up.

In this chapter we'll cover:

- Opening a second store
- Diversifying
- Franchising
- Selling
- Passing the business on to family or friends

➡ OPENING A SECOND STORE

Had Sir Richard Branson decided to call it a day after the first Virgin Records, it's fair to assume he'd be worth several billion less and still shifting CDs for a living instead of plotting passenger space voyages. Likewise, the various retail giants quickly homogenising high streets the length and breadth of the UK all originated from a single shop.

Going multiple has brazen appeal to any entrepreneurially-minded shop owner. At face value, it's a simple equation: if you can sell more, you can buy cheaper, increase margin, reinvest in another store, further reduce costs by centralising backend functions such as accounts, HR, warehousing etc, reinvest in growth; and so on.

If all goes to plan you'll soon have a burgeoning retail empire and a healthy number of envious competitors looking to buy you out, or a pack of eager investors to back you to take it towards a stock market flotation and make you and them a whole pile of cash.

Obstacles along the way

You'll note we've jumped a criminally long way in three paragraphs from shop to public company. That journey happens infrequently enough as it is, and if you factor in the number of times it happens without the original founders departing and a lot of pain along the way it is even rarer.

Aside from the fact most shops don't have the scalable proposition needed to successfully launch multiple shops, that hassle is the main reason most people are happy sticking with what they've got.

Taking on a second store, let alone aiming towards a chain, is full of risk. It's a word we used a lot in the planning stages of the book and it rightly resurfaces with abundance here. All the risk you took on when trying to establish your first shop, find suitable premises, establish a customer base and develop strong supplier relationships are all just as relevant the second time around.

While the upside to scaling a business is that you can reduce your outgoings, you can also double them if anything goes wrong. If there are problems fitting out your second shop which delays opening or the first six months is more difficult than you think, it's the first shop which takes the brunt.

Preparations to make

Before you even consider opening a second store you need to ensure the first is strong enough to take it in several respects. From a cashflow perspective you need to ensure your first shop can sustain the start-up costs of the set-up and then the inevitable losses until it hits breakeven. You also need to account for your absence from the business. If you're spending all your time focussing on shop two, make sure shop one doesn't fall apart. If you haven't got an experienced store manager, then get one before you take yourself away from the business.

The lesson to be taken from both those that have failed and succeeded is to take your time. Perfect the business model at shop one first. Make sure every element from supplier chain to brand message and store layout is optimised until you've got a model you're confident you can replicate at different premises. If this takes five years, let it take five years. It's far easier to expand a working model quickly than a broken one – indeed, you'll almost certainly get to store 10 quicker this way rather than rushing to numbers three or four and watching them fall apart because you're not sufficiently prepared.

Establish and plan out exactly how the business will change. Speak to suppliers to ensure the better rates you're expecting are correct in your business plan, look how you'll be able to centralise accounts and possibly warehousing, plan for staff training etc. Carry out all the usual research you would for a first shop.

> **FROM THE EXPERTS:**
> ## Mike Clare, Dreams
>
> You never really know why a store doesn't work, because you wouldn't open it if you did. We think out of 10, you get one star, one dog and eight that are OK. You just need to hope you don't get a dog in your first two or three because it's far harder to survive than when you've eight or nine to prop you up.

Then think hard about what happens if it goes wrong – because there's a good chance it will. Every entrepreneur who's successfully rolled out a chain of shops, or similarly, restaurants, will have had some that haven't worked – and almost all of them won't be able to tell why they didn't, or what was better about the ones that did.

Throughout the process you should be asking if this is still a good idea and if it's not, then press the pause button and reassess. Expansion can be an exhilarating, exciting phase but it can also be one where you can haemorrhage money and undo so much of the good work you've put in over the past few years, so be careful.

> **IN MY EXPERIENCE:**
>
> ## Clare Thommen, Boudiche
>
> We've the finances in place for a third boutique but the priority for us is to review our systems and processes to ensure we've a slick, stable platform to grow the business on.

It's also worth reassessing why you first opened your shop. For very few people the main motivation for starting any type of business is to make lots of money. More often, it's about the freedom of working for themselves, realising an idea or simply enjoying a richer life than employment previously enabled. For a shop in particular, many people are drawn by the prospect of working in an environment where they're mixing with the public, working with people they've chosen to or in many cases their family.

Necessary changes

Almost always, opening a second or multiple stores changes your role. When you decide to take a shop beyond one store it becomes a serious retail business and you become an entrepreneur more than a shopkeeper and inevitably spend more time in meetings, in the office, out with suppliers or travelling between shops than before. Many people thrive on different type of pressure and responsibility but for others it is the antithesis of why they opened a shop in the first place and is an unwelcome culture shock.

 DIVERSIFYING

A safer way to expand your business is to diversify into new areas. It might be that you decide to widen your offering by selling complimentary items, or find new supplementary channels to sell through.

As with opening a second store, any kind of diversification away from your core business is likely to carry some risk as you'll be directing funds and your energies elsewhere. As such you shouldn't look to diversify too early. Plenty of shops have damaged a profitable and thriving business model by splashing out on a new range of goods that don't work.

If you do diversify into selling other goods, be careful not to dilute your identity or the USPs that make your business unique. For instance, if your shop has established itself by selling premium, organic goods, don't try and cash in by selling cheaper, non-organic products as well. You might bring a few extra passers-by in off the street but will lose your differentiation as a stand out destination for your original target customer.

Multi-channel selling

One of the smartest ways to grow your revenues from pure shop sales is to extend your channels for selling. Indeed almost all successful retail brands are not multi-channel operations.

At a minimum, you should be looking within the first year to 18 months to be selling online as well as from the shop. Why limit your sales to just people that are able to visit you when there's a whole world out there you can sell to? Even shops such as convenience stores serving a small local community can take advantage of the internet, offering delivered groceries or premium services or the ability to settle newspaper accounts online etc.

Selling online will enable you to diversify stock offerings which are impractical for the shop. For example, if you're a small independent garden centre you can offer a wider range of garden furniture online than it's possible to display in the shop.

Similarly, mail order remains a profitable sales channel for many independent shops with similar advantages to web sales.

IN MY EXPERIENCE:
Paul Mathers, Sherston Post Office Stores

We've already added an alcohol license and are looking at relocating over the road to larger premises to incorporate a wine shop into our offering.

The advantage to both channels is that you can provide calls to action to the customer that you're unable to do with a shop: ie you can't force someone to walk past your shop, but you can send them a sales brochure containing all this season's stock or clearance offers and you can do the same online via email mail-outs.

With multi-channel selling in mind, you should be collecting customer data at every opportunity from day one. Run competitions on the counter to give away vouchers for the shop and ask people to fill in quick forms containing their email and home addresses and confirming that it's OK for you to contact them.

As soon as you can afford it, start sending out email and print newsletters saying how much you value their custom, offering useful tips and hints around the subject you specialise in and offering exclusive deals and special offers.

IN MY EXPERIENCE:

Lance Prebble, Pole Position

I don't quite understand how any retailer nowadays isn't multichannel selling. You have to get your money where you can and everything needs to be integrated.

Concessions

Another route to market, and a less risky alternative to opening a second store, is via retail concessions. Increasingly, larger retail outlets and department stores are letting out small areas of their floor space to complimentary brands.

Concessions are a great way to guarantee footfall and piggyback on larger retailers' heritage and marketing spend. A concession in Selfridges in a prime point of London's Oxford Street could catapult your brand to a segment of the shopping public that you couldn't otherwise get near. And of course, there's none of the risk or commitment associated with having your own premises.

As a result, concessions aren't particularly cheap. The prime spots are competitive to start with and can turn into mini auctions. You'll be expected to pay an occupation fee and in many cases a percentage of turnover back to the store. It's likely you'll also have to satisfy the store managing the concession of the quality of the goods you'll be selling and the immediate security of the business.

Concessions can also have backend complications. Some stores like stock to be tagged and labelled with their pricing and alarm system so you may have to change your EPOS system accordingly and make special arrangements with suppliers.

If you think concessions could be for you, take a look around at complimentary stores, speak to other concession holders about the how the deals they've got work and contact the stores directly. Also try concession agencies that manage slots on behalf of stores. One of the largest is: http://www.retailconcessions.co.uk/index.htm

➡ FRANCHISING

What is it?

If you've created a successful new shop concept you may feel it has the potential to work really well as a chain. However, to do this you'll need heavy investment and a lot of hard work. One option for growing your business into a chain without running each site yourself is to turn the concept into a franchise.

A franchise is a successful business blueprint which you can then sell to other people. The franchisees will finance and manage the business, but use the brand, identity and concept you've created. The most famous example of any franchise is probably McDonald's. Other well-known examples in the UK include Thorntons, Prontaprint, Shell petrol stations, Cashconverters and Coffee Republic Deli's.

> IN MY EXPERIENCE:
> ## Lance Prebble, Pole Position
> We're working on making the business model fully exportable so it can be implemented in any similar size retail environment with good footfall; which then makes it a franchiseable product.

How does it work?

If you want to franchise your shop the first thing you need to do is perfect your entire business model – product, supplier chain, sales channels, brand, marketing channels, staff hierarchy and training procedures – to the point it could be easily replicated by anyone else with similar skills to you.

Once you're happy about this there's a clear formalised process to follow. You need to collate a complete business package or manual. Your franchisee buys this from you, but must agree to trade under your company name and abide by whatever trading methods you specify. If you want to, you can stipulate that all products and goods must be bought from you, or a particular supplier. You can also request additional items to be purchased from you including staff uniforms, furniture, marketing materials etc. How much of this is included in your initial fee and package is down to you and the contract you draw up with your franchisees.

The contract between you and your franchisee is very important. It stipulates what ongoing financial obligations they owe to you, and specifies exactly how much influence or control you have over the way they run the shop. However, the franchisee will also require some assurances too. They'll want to know how much support they'll get from you in setting up the business and its ongoing management. They'll probably also expect a degree of marketing to be done by you on the overall brand.

You need to decide how much you want to charge for the initial licensing of the concept. Franchises can cost anything from £5,000 to £500,000 to buy depending on a number of factors ranging from the estimated profit it will generate to the size of the operation. In general though the franchisor (you) should price the franchise sensibly enough so that franchisees can afford the start-up capital to get the shop up and running.

You will then receive ongoing revenue from a share of the turnover of each business. You can also make money from a mark-up of anything you sell to your franchisees.

What you need to do

If you decide to franchise your business the first thing you need to do is go back to the drawing board in terms of research. You need to think long and hard about whether or not your concept is suited to franchising. If you're meticulous about quality control then a franchise may not be the best option for you. However, if you've created a concept that you feel can be successfully managed by others then it's definitely an option to consider.

The British Franchise Association (www.thebfa.org) can give you lots of help and advice in getting your concept off the ground. It's a good idea to contact the organisation early on in your planning stage. There's also a whole channel dedicated to franchising information on Startups.co.uk. You can find useful information on franchising as well list your own shop on the site so potential franchisees can contact you.

Useful franchise resources

The British Franchise Association
www.thebfa.org
01865 379892

FranchiseInfo
www.franinfo.co.uk

How2Franchise
www.how2franchise.co.uk

UK franchise directory
www.theukfranchisedirectory.net

Attracting franchisees

To make a substantial amount from a franchise concept you need to have enough franchisees. Remember, it's only a share of the profits you'll be getting from each business. Your franchisees will need to be able to keep the majority of the revenue otherwise what's in it for them? To gain enough franchisees you need to have an attractive package and market it well. Here's a few tips:

● Your initial fee and ongoing royalties need to be low enough to be affordable and attractive to potential franchisees. However, you need to strike a balance between affordable for them, and profitable for you.
● Your business should also be well established, secure and have an excellent reputation before you even think about franchising. You need to be able to prove to your potential franchisees that it's a business concept worth investing in. The only way to do that is to hone your own operation into a finely tuned concept.

- You need to offer enough management support. It's no good just throwing in the rights to the shop name and a few uniforms. You need a thorough business manual with instructions on everything from products and customer service to floor layouts and prices.
- You need to show a willingness to market and develop the business from a central office. Franchisees are buying into a brand name, with all the security and customer recognition that offers.
- You need to prove you're willing to protect the brand, which means choosing your franchisees carefully. You can't just hand out the licence to anyone willing to stump up the cash. One bad franchise brings down the reputation of all of them, and your hard-working franchisees will want reassurance that their business isn't being undermined by unsuccessful branches.

Franchising can be a hugely effective and efficient way of rolling out your brand but it's also a time-consuming and responsible process. While you're earning revenues from franchisees, you're also trusting them with your brand and that crucial end-user relationship. The profit you'll generate from a chain of shops will never be as great as if you were fully in control either, so there's a call to be made between getting there quickly, or at all, with the help of others, or slowly, or not at all, on your own.

➡ SELLING OR EXITING THE BUSINESS

Should you sell?

There are many reasons why you may feel like selling your shop. You may want to cash in on the financial success of what you've built by accepting an offer from another retailer or an investor. Or perhaps you want to move on, either to a different location or because of family or personal commitments. Or maybe you just want to retire. Building up a successful business that can be sold on may have been your intention from the very beginning. Whatever your reasons for wanting to sell, there are plenty of things to consider before you do so.

Another reason you may consider selling your business is if it's not performing as well as expected. If your shop is in financial difficulty a sale could prove tricky. However, it may be a way of recouping some of your investment without closing it down altogether. If this is the case, you should prepare yourself for price offers that don't reflect the amount of time, effort and money you've put into the business.

The most likely option for selling a single shop is in a trade sale to another retailer or business owner. However, if the shop you've built up is big and profitable enough, you may find that a private equity buyer or venture capital firm is interested.

Preparing to sell

Selling your business takes a lot of planning. It's not as simple as handing over the keys in exchange for a cheque. It needs to be in a sale-ready state which means making sure all your finances are in immaculate order. The same goes for the whole business operation. The books need to have been gone through with a fine toothcomb. Needless to say, all tax and official records must be completely up to date. You'll also need to be able to produce evidence of cashflow, turnover and profits. This will apply to the financial history of the business as well as how it's currently performing and what your projections for the future are.

Before you even think about selling your business it's a good idea to take on some help in the form of an accountant and a solicitor. Your accountant should be able to prepare the business accounts for a sale. You may already have an accountant, but if they are not experienced when it comes to business sales it's advisable to bring somebody on board who is. Your solicitor will be the one responsible for drafting sale agreements and will negotiate with your buyer and their legal advisors if necessary.

Valuing your business

There are so many different factors that affect the value of your business, and your current turnover and profit is just one part of that. Essentially your business is only worth what buyers are willing to pay. This can be affected by things that are beyond your control such as the current state of the economy, the value of property in the area and what similar businesses are going on the market for.

However, there are plenty more elements of your business that will have been shaped and controlled by you. These include:

- Financial history
- Current financial health
- The shop's reputation

- The shop's position within the community
- The potential for growth
- The quality of your team
- The contents and physical appearance of your shop

Part of presenting a valuation of your shop to potential buyers will involve preparing a sales memorandum. This will generally be produced in conjunction with your sales advisors – ie your accountant and solicitor. The sales memorandum is a kind of marketing pitch which includes information on your company, and presents it in a favourable light in order to attract buyers. Information on the memorandum includes trading history, key financial figures and how these have fared during previous years. The memorandum will also have details on your premises and your employees.

Finding buyers

Potential buyers are everywhere. You may be able to target a competitor in your area that's keen to take over your business and expand their own. Or maybe you know someone who runs a similar business in another location that's keen to take on an extra business. If you're considering selling your shop you may want to return to good old fashioned networking to find potential buyers. You can even look within your own team for a buyer. Perhaps one of your staff members is in a position to stump up the cash to take over your shop.

However, if you don't know someone personally that's in a position to buy your business you'll have to advertise that it's for sale. There are several trade magazines and business directories you can use to list your shop in. These include:

- Daltons Business: www.daltonsbusiness.com
- Businesses For Sale: www.businessesforsale.com

Once you have some interested buyers that you feel are realistically in a position to take your shop over, you can have your advisors send them your sales memorandum. You don't have to meet all of your potential buyers at this stage, but obviously with a business such as a shop, it's likely they'll want to view it before making any kind of initial offer. If you have several interested buyers, the next stage will be to start holding meetings with them.

> ### ✦ TIP
> It's a good idea to draw up a non-disclosure agreement for all prospective buyers to sign. This way, even if you have to reveal confidential company information to them, you can be confident they won't reveal it to anyone else.

Choosing a buyer

Choosing a buyer should never just be a question of accepting the highest bid. You should also consider how your buyer is willing to structure the sale, to what extent they are planning to change or build on what you've already developed and what you both agree is an acceptable timetable for finalising the sale.

Once you've agreed a sale with your buyer it will then be subject to the process of due diligence. This is where the buyer engages in a thorough inspection of the business, covering things such as financial records, staff agreements, customer and supplier relationships, premises, legal and tax obligations and intellectual property.

Your responsibility

If you're selling your shop you need to be aware of Transfer of Undertakings (Protection of Employment) Regulations 2006, also known as TUPE. You'll be familiar with these regulations if you bought your business from someone else. The basis of these regulations are that when a business changes hands, the new employer is not allowed to change the terms of employment the existing members of staff currently have. All your employees, or at least a representative of them, should also be consulted and informed regarding the sale of your business.

When you sell a business you also have a responsibility to the taxman to consider. Entrepreneurs are subject to Capital Gains Tax (CGT) when they sell off business assets. In 2008 changes to CGT came into force which included the abolition of Taper Relief which allowed assets held for more than two years to enjoy a reduced rate of 10%. Gains made on the disposal of business assets are now charged at a flat rate of 18%. There are a few exceptions however.

TIP

If your gains are equal to, or less than, the annual exempt amount, you may not have to pay CGT. The annual exempt amount for 2008/09 is £9,600. Another exemption applies where your lifetime gains do not exceed £1m. This is called entrepreneurs' relief, and it charges gains at a reduced rate of 10%. Any gains after your first £1m are charged at 18%.

There are other allowances and exemptions to CGT which is why it is advisable to seek professional advice from a specialised accountant or solicitor before you sell your business.

Passing the business on to a friend or relative

If you decide you want to sell the business to a friend or relative, the same process as above will still apply. However, you may want to pass the business on, perhaps to a son or daughter, without receiving payment for it. The first thing you need to consider is whether the person you've earmarked for taking over the shop is really suited to doing so. If they've worked with you in the shop, it should be pretty apparent whether or not they're capable of taking over all your responsibilities. However, if they don't have the right level of experience, and we've established by now that running a shop is definitely not a business anyone can come along and make a success of, you could find all your hard work goes out the door as soon as you hand over the keys.

TIP

There may also be Capital Gains Tax implications involved in passing the business on to a family member even if you're not selling it, so it's important you take sound advice from a specialist accountant and solicitor before you hand the business over.

As well as assessing whether or not your successor is capable of taking over the business, you also need to establish if they even want to. Running a shop takes passion and dedication and if you pass the business on to someone who's taken it over out of a sense of obligation, your shop could soon suffer the consequences. Another possible problem, particularly when passing a business on to offspring is making a decision about who has overall control and responsibility. If you have more than one child, you may want them both to share in the financial success of the business, but conflict could arise if you haven't established from the outset who has overall control when it comes to management decisions.

The same goes for your own involvement. How much day to day involvement do you still want, and will whoever you've passed the business on to be comfortable with that? It's no good handing over the responsibility and hard work of the shop management to somebody, only to enforce your own decisions on the business. If you really want to pass the business on to somebody else, you need to be willing to let go of the reins.

Things to remember:

- Business development isn't just about increasing your profits. It's also about maintaining quality and improving what you've already built.

- Don't take on extra responsibility if it puts the health of the shop at risk.

- Don't consider a second shop until you feel you can be away from your first one without it collapsing.

- Franchising demands a flawless original business model. Don't consider this route until you've achieve one.

- Make sure you take professional advice before beginning a transfer or sale of the shop.

Appendices

SWOT analysis table

Strengths	Weaknesses
• Why should you succeed? • What do you do well? • Why do customers say they enjoy doing business with you? • What distinct advantages does your company offer? • What are your USPs?	• What could be improved about the business? • Is the market strong enough? • Do you have enough/good enough staff on board? • Are your management skills up to scratch? • Do you have enough finance to make it work? • What stumbling blocks do you continue to encounter? • What does your company do that can be improved? • What should be avoided? • What do your competitors do better than you?
S	**W**
Opportunities **O**	**T** **Threats**
• Where are the openings for your business? • Has the market significantly changed recently? • What customer needs are not being met by your competitors?	• What is your competition doing that could take business away from you or stunt your company's growth? • How might your competitors react to any moves you make? • What trends in the market do you see that could wipe you out or make your business obsolete? • Might technology changes threaten your products or services? Or your job? • Do you have a stable relationship with suppliers and partners?

Example market analysis table for a new trendy clothes shop on a busy town high street

Competitors	Number of years established	Price bracket (eg cost of main meal)	Their strengths	Their weaknesses	Your USPs/what you offer the market
Small shop, selling low-end clothes	5	£10	Good for a quick buy, popular with younger girls	Quality of clothes is questionable, sparse decor	Fresh, inviting décor, with well-priced, quality goods
Chain clothes shop	8	£40	Well established and good reputation. Very busy.	Lacking in choice? Limited by the chain's lines. Impersonal service	Well-trained, attentive staff. Discount on second visit.
Boutique shop	3	£70	The high-end choice, very nice clothes, nice décor. Attentive, but not pushy staff	Rarely very busy, appeals to a very niche market	Aim to create the same friendly atmosphere, but with mid-range goods to ensure a wider appeal.

Financial budget plan

Startup costs	Estimated cost
Business registration fees	
Initial stock	
Rent deposits	
Down payments on property	
Down payments on equipment	
Shopfitting costs	
Utility set up fees	
Operating costs	
Your salary	
Staff salaries	
Rent or mortgage payments	
Telecommunications	
Utlities	
Stock	
Storage	
Distribution	
Promotion	
Loan payments	
Office supplies	
Maintenance	
Professional services (ie accountancy fees)	